SHAKESPEAREAN

REPRESENTATION

Shakespearean Representation

Mimesis and Modernity in Elizabethan Tragedy

BY HOWARD FELPERIN

PRINCETON UNIVERSITY PRESS

PRINCETON, NEW JERSEY

Copyright © 1977 by Princeton University Press
Published by Princeton University Press,
Princeton, New Jersey
In the United Kingdom: Princeton University Press,
Guildford, Surrey

All Rights Reserved

Library of Congress Cataloging in Publication Data will
be found on the last printed page of this book

This book has been composed in Linotype Baskerville

Printed in the United States of America
by Princeton University Press,
Princeton, New Jersey

For my brother Karl,
whose delight in interpretation
of the text of our lives
exceeds my own

ACKNOWLEDGMENTS

SEVERAL of the following chapters were first delivered as lectures before gatherings at various universities. Chapter two was presented at the Renaissance Colloquy, Yale University, in March, 1971, and again at the Conference on British Studies, Holy Cross University, in April, 1971. It subsequently appeared under the title, "O'erdoing Termagant: An Approach to Shakespearean Mimesis" in *The Yale Review*, Spring, 1974, © Yale University. I wish to thank the editors for permission to reprint. The opening chapter was delivered in successive versions at the Comparative Literature Colloquium, Yale University, April, 1972; at the UCLA Conference on Contemporary Criticism, March, 1973; and at the University of Connecticut, November, 1974. Chapter four, on *Macbeth*, was presented before the Department of English at the University of Kansas in March, 1975. To my hosts and audiences goes my gratitude for the valuable criticism and encouragement these occasions generated. An A.C.L.S. grant for the academic year 1974-75 enabled me to complete the writing of the book in substantially its present form.

The difficulty of sorting out more intimate and extensive indebtednesses is particularly acute for a book whose preoccupations are those not merely of its author but of several others with whom its author has had a running dialogue over the past ten years. My close friend and colleague David Thorburn could always be counted on to provide the most loyal, cogent, and fructifying opposition on all matters pertaining to literature and life. A. Bartlett Giamatti and Leslie Brisman each read portions of the manuscript and offered valuable advice. Michael Gagarin cast a professional eye over all matters relating to Latin and Greek texts. The speculations of Geoffrey Hartman on

Acknowledgments

literary history have been continually provocative. The fact that I, like everyone else, take issue with the recent work of Harold Bloom on poetic influence, in no way nullifies the force of that work or the debt I owe him. Finally, the pervasive influence of Paul de Man upon this book must be so apparent to those familiar with his work as to be embarrassing to me and perhaps to him.

CONTENTS

Acknowledgments	vii
Preface	3
1. The Poetics of Modernity: Homer and Others	12
2. O'erdoing Termagant: *Hamlet*	44
3. Plays Within Plays: *Othello, King Lear, Antony and Cleopatra*	68
4. A Painted Devil: *Macbeth*	118
5. "Jacobean Decadence": Tourneur, Middleton, Webster, Ford	145
Index	197

SHAKESPEAREAN

REPRESENTATION

PREFACE

THIS is a book about the modernity of certain older poets and the way that modernity is realized in the work of one of them. Obviously there is a paradox here that requires some explanation. On the one hand, we are often told that Shakespeare is "our contemporary" and that certain of his plays are particularly of or for "our time." Yet, on the other, we insist on the Elizabethan quality of his work as the product and reflection of a culture very different and remote from our own. How is it that Shakespeare can be both our contemporary and an Elizabethan, of our time and his own? And how can so charged and fashionable a term as "modernity" be applied to his plays in conjunction with such old-fashioned and, as some might say, antithetical terms as "representation" and "mimesis"? Does not literary modernity, at least in its most recent phase, imply the doing away with traditional, i.e., classical and renaissance, notions of art as imitation?

The problem at its most general is formulated in a recent work on modern literature, a work I came upon after completing the present study, but one that bears directly on the issues it raises. "Our awareness," writes Lionel Trilling, "of the difference between the moral assumptions of one culture and those of another is so developed and active that we find it hard to believe there is any such thing as an essential human nature; but we all know moments when these differences, as literature attests to them, seem to make no difference, seem scarcely to exist. We read the *Iliad* or the plays of Sophocles or Shakespeare and they come so close to our hearts and minds that they put to rout, or into abeyance, our instructed consciousness of the moral life as it is conditioned by a particular culture—they persuade us that human nature never varies, that the moral life is

Preface

unitary and its terms perennial, and that only a busy intruding pedantry could ever have suggested otherwise."[1] The fact that Trilling himself, in pursuing the argument that classic modern literature reflects just such a "mutation" in moral sensibility, falls back on the very premise of cultural and historical difference he has put into question does not lay to rest the doubts he has raised about its validity. Which of us, after all, while thinking to understand the works of the past, and ourselves through them, by documenting these differences would unwittingly turn into a busy, intruding, and Polonian pedant?

This passage of eloquent doubt voices the uncertain sense of the relations between literary history and literary modernity that underlies all our scholarly labors, however loving. And it is particularly, almost poignantly, relevant to our dealings with older or classic literature, where the assumption of historical and cultural difference is most deeply ingrained. No more than Trilling would I confidently deny the existence of the manifold differences between Elizabethan literature and culture and our own, or dismiss the devoted labors of the generations of scholars who have documented them. But, like Trilling, I find myself increasingly doubtful, as an historical interpreter, about the importance for literary understanding of all these undeniable differences. For the meaning of literature, as the grammatical tense in which we discuss authors and texts implies, must always be present. Does it really matter to our effort at understanding *Macbeth* that the culture within which Shakespeare wrote held different views of religion, government, psychology—of virtually any aspect of social and individual existence we may care to name—and that these different views are everywhere reflected in the play?

Even if a composite Elizabethan sense of the world could be recovered or reconstructed, would it really be of value to us? And would it really be Shakespeare's, as dis-

[1] *Sincerity and Authenticity* (Cambridge, Mass., 1972), pp. 1-2.

Preface

tinct from some typical or hypothetical Elizabethan's? The effort of what I term in the pages that follow an archeological or conservative or pious criticism, with its basis in assumed cultural difference and its aspiration toward a nostalgic or antiquarian recovery of "original" meaning, largely ignores such questions. Nor does it stop to ask how plays so preoccupied with, say, kings can still touch the lives of men who have nothing to do with monarchs or monarchy? It cannot explain, much less encourage, Shakespeare's uncanny capacity to speak with most miraculous organ across his cultural separation from us in a language which is still understandable with minimal instruction, and which still conveys the fluent urgency that Trilling, among many others, hears in it. Such an archeological criticism, in sum, denies Shakespeare's present meaning and continuing modernity—the reason, after all, he is still read, taught, and produced—and renders up instead a museum piece. Needless to say, this is the very opposite of what we, as wellmeaning historical scholars, intended in the first place.

Yet neither is Shakespeare's perennial modernity to be located in some unique or special affinity between this playwright or this or that of his plays and contemporary readers and theatergoers. Some congruence of this kind is usually what is being argued for or assumed when critics write of Shakespeare as "our contemporary" or of one or another of his plays as "in our time"—as if he were more *our* contemporary than some other audience's, or other plays of his were *less* of our time than this or that one. Such elective affinities and special relationships are usually based on alleged resemblances between the theme or mood of a given Shakespearean play and the themes and mood which are supposed to characterize modern, i.e., twentieth-century literature—the by now familiar complex of such informing ideas as absurdity, nihilism, alienation, *Angst*, and so on. Although the sense of the world evoked by these commonplaces can no doubt be found in Shakespeare's work, and not exclusively in his tragedies, his modernity can hardly

Preface

be said to reside in an historical thematic more or less prefigurative or even prophetic of that of twentieth-century art. It would scarcely be "modern" of Shakespeare to tell us what we know, or think we know, already and more fully. As his own contemporary saw with absolute clarity, Shakespeare was not of his time or ours but "for all time," no more of this age or that age than of some other, no less "modern" for ages that did not or will not define themselves by the particular set of conventions and commonplaces we take, perhaps over-confidently, to define our own.

The literary modernity of which Shakespearean tragedy serves as a paradigm in the ensuing chapters is not conceived of as primarily a chronological or period matter. For in this most simple and straightforward usage of the term, as a synonym for "recent" or "contemporary" or "twentieth-century," the idea of the "modern" harbors more than enough difficulties to put into question its usefulness in describing our experience of the immediacy of "classic" authors. Those who have written, for example, of "the modern tradition" or of "classic modern literature" do not always seem to be fully aware of the tensions implicit in such attempts to combine an idea of historical remoteness with an idea of temporal immediacy. Quite apart from actual or potential disagreements over just which "modern" authors and texts constitute the "tradition" and are to be considered "classic," is there not something altogether too obliging about a modernism that can be so easily reconciled with the idea of a "tradition" or assimilated to a "classic" status? Some have realized that the innovative, even aggressive or defiant, constituent of any true literary modernity is lost or compromised in the idea of classic modern literature or of a modern tradition and would re-locate those qualities in the movement of "post-modernism," a designation intended to call attention to what is new and adventurous in recent writing and distinguish it in fact from a modernism that now seems tame and traditional. Of course this is only to perpetuate the same error of trying to

Preface

explain the unknown by the more unknown, for how can we talk of "post-modernism" when the nature of modernism itself is still very much open to question? Will the same critics soon be talking of "post-post-modernism" to distinguish the writing of the near future from that "post-modern" literature which will itself already have passed into tradition and become classic? Clearly, there is an impulse within the literary modernity of any period that transcends mere chronicity and resists identification, at least for very long, with what is most recent.

In what, then, does this elusive but apparently ineluctable modernity of classic authors consist if it is not a matter of chronology or period? It is rather, as my subtitle suggests and the ensuing chapters will attempt to show, a function of the mimetic process itself. Modernity and mimesis are both inextricably implicated in the traditional, and if we stop to think about it, root sense of literature as "representation." In any re-presentation, that is, an idea of imitation, repetition, and continuity is combined with a contrary idea of innovation, differentiation, and discontinuity. The notion that literary modernity always stands in a necessary structural relation to mimesis may strike many as quaint, particularly since modernist and post-modernist writing is often said nowadays to have taken leave, or to be in the process of taking leave, of mimesis as a bourgeois and atavistic fetish, in favor of a more purely intransitive or reflexive activity emptied of external reference. In this view, "realism" and related literary movements are merely an aberration in the history of literature. This is not the place to enter upon the complex theoretical issues that dominate contemporary literary study, especially since the book itself is implicitly embroiled in them throughout, and will have to bear its own complex witness to them. Suffice it to say at this point that the view of literature as a self-referential structure, in which mimesis and modernity are incompatible concepts, is based on a misunderstanding of the former as well as the latter.

Preface

For mimesis, the illusion of reality traditionally ascribed to literature in general and epitomized in Shakespeare's plays, arises not from the direct imitation of "nature" or "life" or "experience" but, as I try to show, from the *re-presentation*, with a difference, of inherited models or constructs of "nature," "life," and "experience." For the notion of "re-presentation," as something distinct from a presentation on the one hand and from a copy on the other, depends, like the notion of modernity, on the idea of difference after all. This difference, however, is not primarily cultural and historical but literary. It designates precisely that impulse within the greatest literature of every age to depart from all such prior reconstructions of experience, to leave behind its own literary and conventional mediations, to shed its mediated status altogether, and thereby join with and become experience itself, i.e., that which is not literature. The most truly modern work would thus, in theory, also and simultaneously be the most truly mimetic, since both modernity and mimesis seek ultimately to break through or away from the mediations of art and become spontaneous and unprecedented "life." It is in this sense that Shakespearean tragedy can fairly be called "modern" and "mimetic" without contradiction, at least as modern and mimetic as literature has ever succeeded in becoming.

A given Shakespearean play thus demands a conservative or archeological response in so far as it carries within itself an archaic or received sign-system—miracle play, revenge play, historical morality—whose codes, being things of culture and history, are remote from us and require deciphering. Hence the present study is not without pedantry. But the same play makes a further and more strenuous demand. It requires, if we are to arrive at a present meaning, a romantic or modernist response as well, in so far as it insists on its own difference from that older sign-system, its departure from prior art in the direction of present life. Thus it is that *Macbeth*, for example, can still engage us today for all its preoccupation with kings and kingship, which are, if

Preface

taken literally, merely the signs or badges of a vanished cultural and historical moment. But kings and kingship carry more than temporal, local, and literal meaning; they are free or floating signifiers for which every age and reader may discover, as Macbeth himself does to his surprise, an unpredetermined significance beyond that which they hold in the play's inherited and inscribed models.

This process of discovery that signs, roles, forms mean something more or other than what they have been presupposed to mean is, of course, nothing other than interpretation. But because interpretation always implies a gap between sign and significance, between "original" and present meaning—a gap into which the interpreter must descend and within which the risky work of interpretation is carried out—it is no wonder that it is often viewed with mistrust by those archeological scholars who wish to rest on the side of a secure older meaning. From this viewpoint, interpretation always looks something like a fall, a continuing and bottomless fall into subjectivity, into secularity, into all that we think of as modernity in the sense of a poor and unhappy thing, but our own. For the fall into interpretation, as experienced by Shakespeare's heroes or their interpreters, though it may be a heady or exhilarating trauma, is like all falls tragic in its essence and therefore to be avoided, if possible, in the interest of self-preservation. This may be why there is so much commentary on Shakespeare's tragedies and so little genuine interpretation.

The felt discrepancy I have been describing, between the established and stable forms of prior art and the life they can but stiffly gesture toward, lies at the heart of Shakespearean tragedy, the source of its unparalleled mimetic illusionism and continuing modernity alike. But at the same time, the deliberate and self-conscious process by which the inadequacies of prior convention are revealed, though central to these plays' illusion of reality and their protagonists' assertions of authentic selfhood, may itself be seen as no more than another artistic convention. What begins as a

Preface

revelation of the mediated status of prior art in the interest of engaging life directly becomes one more mediation to be revealed and repudiated as such by the playwrights who follow Shakespeare in the continuing process of representation. Shakespeare's own tragedies, that is, are subject to the same process of mimetic revision as medieval and Tudor dramatic forms had been subjected within his tragedies. This restless dialectic between convention and the repudiation of convention in the name of reality, between imitation and innovation, may thus be seen as the basis of literary history, since these fluctuations can be traced not only within Shakespeare's plays but in relation to the drama that precedes and follows them, the drama they inscribe and the drama that inscribes them.

The result is a series of interpretations of the major tragedies of Shakespeare's age that is also a model for reconstructing from within the genre a literary history of the genre. The main advantage of such a model is that unlike most forms of literary historiography it is not conceived as a rigid structure external to the works it discusses and prejudicing our response to them. In traditional literary history, that is, we begin with a certain historical scheme into which a given work is then fitted so as to yield an "historical" reading that confirms the expectations and presuppositions implicit in our original scheme. There is a certain circularity, for example, in reading Shakespeare as a "renaissance playwright" when what constitutes a renaissance playwright has been assumed in advance and is then sought in his plays, or in reading the major Jacobeans in terms of an alleged historical "decadence," the main evidence for which is their plays. Such circularities, with the diminishment of artistic voluntarism and individuality they imply, can be avoided if literary history is conceived not as the begetter of interpretations but as the byproduct of interpretation. For literary history, from the point of view of the poet, is necessarily a flexible, even collapsible, structure, which is carried about within a given work in the form of a

Preface

particular set of allusions to prior works and which can be reconstructed only through the process of interpretation.

The approach to literary historiography adumbrated here has a number of potential benefits beyond this obvious one of re-integrating literary history with literary interpretation. Because it focuses on the principles that inform the particularities of literary change, it could also help to bring the study of older literature into closer touch with a methodological reappraisal largely confined at present to the study of later literature. Though I have generally tried to avoid, for reasons of accessibility, the technical terminology in which that reappraisal is being carried out—or more accurately, tried to translate it whenever possible into the traditional vocabulary of literary and dramatic criticism—the present approach may help toward closing still another widening gap within contemporary literary studies. That admittedly overweening and doubtful ambition is to mediate between the peremptory claims of a formal understanding of literature as a synchronic order sustained by its own laws and an historical understanding of literature as a diachronic process unfolding in history and culture. Although the approach offered here no doubt errs in favoring, for corrective purposes, the former, it by no means rules out the possibility of reconstructing and reconciling the latter.

New Haven, Connecticut
August, 1976

CHAPTER 1

The Poetics of Modernity: Homer and Others

> There is nothing in literature but change and change is mockery.
> —William Carlos Williams

MORE than twenty-five years ago, René Wellek and Austin Warren characterized most existing histories of literature as "either social histories, or histories of thought as illustrated in literature, or impressions and judgments on specific works arranged in more or less chronological order." They went on to question whether it is "*possible* to write literary history, that is, to write that which will be both literary and a history."[1] More recently, the question of the possibility and status of literary historiography has arisen again, particularly in the area of romantic and post-romantic studies. "We are all disenchanted," writes Geoffrey Hartman, "with those picaresque adventures in pseudo-causality which go under the name of literary history, those handbooks with footnotes which claim to sing of the whole but load every rift with glue."[2] And Paul de Man argues in a similar vein: "It is generally admitted that a positivistic history of literature, treating it as if it were a collection of empirical data, can only be a history of what literature is not. At best, it would

---

[1] *Theory of Literature* (New York, 1949), ch. 19.
[2] *Beyond Formalism* (New Haven, 1970), p. 356. The essay quoted here, entitled "Toward Literary History," first appeared in *Daedalus*, vol. 99 (1969), no. 2, an issue devoted entirely to the theory of literary history. This renewed attention to an old problem was soon followed by the appearance of a new journal, appropriately entitled *New Literary History*, in 1970.

be a preliminary classification opening the way for actual literary study, and at worst, an obstacle in the way of literary understanding."[3] Despite the efforts of Hartman, de Man, and other romanticists to awaken us to the challenge and difficulty of writing literary history more truly, the urgency of the project and the disenchantment with previous approaches may not be so generally admitted as they suggest, particularly not among scholars who deal with older literatures and nowhere less so than among renaissance scholars.

Although recent efforts to understand Romanticism as more a continuing artistic crisis than a period or a movement have generated probing redefinitions of such traditional concepts as "influence" and "modernity" and quickened speculation on the theory and methodology of literary history, most scholars still take for granted the large historical and structural contours of classical, medieval, and renaissance literature. With marginal adjustments and revisions, such reductive idealizations as "the medieval mind" and "the Elizabethan world-picture" and their variants are alive and well in the pages of the learned journals. We like to think our maps of those earlier literatures, somewhat like actual renaissance maps of the known world, are in more or less reliable agreement, while in the area of romantic and post-romantic literature, every man is his own mapmaker, no two maps conform, and the adventure of charting unknown regions is here. The polemical purpose of the present chapter is to suggest that these attitudes, themselves a romantic legacy, might well be reversed; that our maps of later literary history are arriving at an underlying conformity, while those of earlier literary history are full of unrecognized perils.

Why renaissance studies rests content with an idealized version of its literary history, given the richness of its texts and the turbulence of their cultural context, is outside my immediate concern—unless the very combination of richness

[3] *Blindness and Insight* (New York, 1971), pp. 162-163.

The Poetics of Modernity

and remoteness that period embodies (as opposed to the more fitful genius and relative proximity of Romanticism) invites idealization. But whatever has conditioned the pastoral tranquility of renaissance studies, the fact remains that we now have one kind of literary history for older literature and another kind for later literature, the former generally stressing the benign conservatism of tradition and the latter the innovative anxiety of individual genius. Is this present division in the way we conceive and construct literary history really necessary, a function of some radical difference between two bodies of literature, or is a more unified theory of literary history possible? Phrased more generally, does the ground of change in the arts itself change from epoch to epoch, or is there an underlying ground of change in the arts of all times and places, itself the only constant?

Among recent speculation on literary history originating in romantic studies none is more provocative than the parallel but independent theories of W. J. Bate and Harold Bloom. "The remorseless deepening of self consciousness," writes Bate, "before the rich and intimidating legacy of the past, has become the greatest single problem that modern art (art, that is to say, since the later seventeenth century) has had to face."[4] The continuity of romantic and modern literature, in Bate's view, consists precisely in their foreboding of imminent discontinuity, in the post-seventeenth-century writer's sense of frustration before a formidable past he fears himself inadequate to move beyond. It is this problematic that provides the methodology for a truly modern literary history: "I have often wondered whether we could find any more comprehensive way of taking up the whole of English poetry during the last three centuries—or for that matter the modern history of the arts in general—than by exploring the effects of this accumulating anxiety and the question it so directly presents to the poet or artist: *What is*

[4] *The Burden of the Past and the English Poet* (Cambridge, Mass., 1970), p. 4.

Homer and Others

there left to do?"[5] In Harold Bloom's complementary study of poetic influence (even gloomier than Bate's because it locates the source of crisis in the sad inevitability of continuity rather than the fear of discontinuity), this cumulative anxiety results in the increasing inhibition of poetic genius by its own consciousness of belatedness—particularly in the post-romantic period when the romantics themselves become jealous and terrible father-figures. Bloom's version of the question on which literary history has moved would thus be even more elegiac than Bate's, closer to that framed by Frost's oven-bird: "What to make of a diminished thing?"

For all their timeliness, both theories are actually less novel than they might seem or wish to be. The issue of modernity as an unhappy or problematic condition is at least as old as the literary wars of seventeenth-century France and England between ancients and moderns. And the subjective focus and anguished tonality of both studies distinctly recall their origins in the *Fruhromantik* of Schiller and Friedrich Schlegel, for whom the difficulties of poetic vocation in the modern, i.e., romantic, as opposed to the classical and renaissance, epoch were also a matter of concern. But even if it were demonstrated that Bate's and Bloom's theories of literary history and influence are already implicit in the writings of their romantic precursors, such a demonstration of epigonism would serve only to confirm rather than disconfirm their theories by illustrating their very point within the history of post-romantic literary criticism as a sub-genre of literature proper. To question the special nature of their theories would be more potentially revealing. For common to the writings of Bate and Bloom, as well as Schiller and Schlegel before them, is the assumption that the poet's lot of burden and anxiety before the literary past is an exclusively or especially romantic and post-romantic phenomenon. As Bloom puts it, "Milton [not to mention Shakespeare or Spenser]—as both Johnson and

[5] *The Burden of the Past*, p. 3.

The Poetics of Modernity

Hazlitt emphasize—was incapable of suffering the anxiety of influence, unlike all of his descendents."[6] But is there not internal contradiction, or at least tension, in a theory that confines itself to a time-bound historical era while utilizing the timeless psychological matrix that such concepts as "the burden of the past" and "the anxiety of influence" imply?

No doubt there are reasons why Johnson, Hazlitt, and others emphasize the relative freedom from anxiety of the renaissance past, reasons which will emerge later; yet their emphasis is demonstrably a distortion of that past, and a revealing distortion. It could be shown, for example, that in his casting about for a mode of action, his trying on and putting off of roles handed down by contending literary traditions—classical and medieval—Hamlet's dilemma is also the renaissance poet's. Though the effort of sixteenth-century humanism to classicize English vernacular literature did not succeed, it did present the English poet with an expanded set of available models for tragedy, comedy, epic, and pastoral. But to widen options is always to sharpen the anxiety of choice. The question, academic now, that dominates Elizabethan criticism—to rhyme or not to rhyme?—reflects the anterior and larger question of which models to adopt, vernacular or classical? Sidney's great expectations for English literature, expressed in the *Apology for Poetry*, are dampened only by the persistence of native elements in the productions of his countrymen. He finds much to like for example, in Spenser's *Shepherd's Calendar*; yet "that same framing of his style to an old rustic language I dare not allow, since neither Theocritus in Greek, Virgil in Latin, nor Sannazzaro in Italian did affect it." *Gorboduc* is admi-

---

[6] "Clinamen, or Poetic Misprision," *New Literary History*, I (1970), 3. By the time this essay was reprinted in his fuller study, *The Anxiety of Influence* (New York, 1973), Bloom had begun to backdate the appearance of that anxiety: "Shakespeare belongs to the giant age before the flood, before the anxiety of influence became central to poetic consciousness. . . . Milton, with all his strength, yet had to struggle, subtly and crucially, with a major precursor in Spenser" (p. 11).

rable in "climbing to the height of Seneca's style . . . yet in truth it is very defective in the circumstances, which grieveth me, because it might not remain as an exact model of all tragedies."[7] Spenser's choice of vernacular above classical models incurred the disapproval of Gabriel Harvey's frivolous humanism—"hobgoblin run away with the garland from Apollo"—and Ben Jonson's weightier humanism—"Spenser writ no language"—alike.[8] Even the youthful Milton, retrospectively the most self-confident of poets and always (as Jonson would say) "emulous of the Ancients," deliberates before attempting his epic of epics "whether the rules of Aristotle herein are strictly to be kept, or nature to be followed."[9] Although it might be anachronistic to project onto the renaissance poet the exquisite tortures of the romantic laboring under the "burden of the past" (mainly the renaissance past), it is no less so to pastoralize the Renaissance, that "golden age" of most literary histories, to the extent of emptying it of all analogous burdens and anxieties. Given that the world was all before them, where to choose their models was by no means an academic question. There was anxiety even in Eden. Bate and Bloom fall into error as literary historians in the readiness with which they accept a romantic version of the past for the past itself and proceed to erect their theories of history and influence upon it.

Let us reconsider the crucial case of Milton. Far from being immune to the anxiety of influence, Milton, in his long hesitation before the epic models available to him, may well be its classic and most instructive example. Of the ninety-nine tentative subjects jotted down in the Cambridge manuscript, over a third are from British history and

[7] Sir Philip Sidney, *The Defense of Poesy*, ed. Albert S. Cook (Boston, 1890), p. 47.

[8] "Three proper and wittie familiar Letters," excerpted in *The Complete Poetical Works of Edmund Spenser*, ed. R. E. Neil Dodge (Boston, 1908), p. 773; *Timber, or Discoveries*, in *Ben Jonson*, ed. C. H. Herford, Percy and Evelyn Simpson (Oxford, 1947), vol. VIII, p. 618.

[9] *The Reason of Church Government Urged*, in *The Student's Milton*, ed. Frank Allen Patterson (New York, 1947), p. 525.

The Poetics of Modernity

"Scotch stories, or rather British of the north parts." His note on Alfred is particularly suggestive: "A Heroicall Poem may be founded somewhere in Alfred's reigne, especially at his issuing out of Edelingsey on the Danes; whose actions are well like those of Ulysses." In his Latin verses to Manso, it is no longer Alfred but Arthur and "the magnanimous heroes of the Round Table, invincible by their mutual loyalty" (*invictae sociali foedere mensae / Magnanimos Heroas*) that attract his epic aspirations.[10] The epithet "*magnanimos*" recalls one of Virgil's favorite sobriquets for Aeneas, but it also recalls that "magnificence" which forms the controlling ethical ideal of Spenser's epic and which his Prince Arthur embodies. Indeed, the poem Milton projects cannot help but recall, in its argument and implied form, *The Faerie Queene*. Many reasons have been adduced why Milton never wrote his *Arthuriad* or *Alfrediad* or any national epic in "gothic" form—his anti-monarchical views, his religious bias, the lack of historical documentation—but is it not at least equally possible he did not write that poem because in a sense it had already been written? Moreover, it had been well written. Had not Spenser, the native poet whom he most admired and whose ethical stance he found unimpeachable, effectively exhausted that epic mode? But if Spenser (himself committed to "o'ergoing Ariosto") had preempted one epic convention and made it his own by choosing hobgoblin over Apollo, he left the other open. And this one, the classical epic mode, Milton could and does make truly his own. By sweeping aside the Homeric and Virgilian modes of heroic action—"Thus they relate, / Erring"—Milton makes imaginative room for himself to sing "the better fortitude / Of patience and heroic martyrdom" hitherto unsung, while making sure to retain an echo of those earlier modes. The classical as opposed to the vernacular epic was useful to Milton in precisely the degree to which its earlier uses could be discredited.

[10] *The Student's Milton*, pp. 1131, 144.

Homer and Others

Milton's poetic situation, that is, had already changed from what Spenser's had been, a major element of that change being the existence of Spenser himself. For even though Spenser also had a rich and diverse epic tradition to contend with at the time he composed his *Faerie Queene*, it was not a tradition in English. What united those Elizabethans who set out to extend native traditions, such as Spenser, and those who wished to follow classical and neoclassical example, such as Sidney and Jonson, was a common desire to establish a literature in English at least comparable to that of "insolent Greece and haughty Rome." The Spenser of *The Shepherd's Calendar* and even of *The Faerie Queene* could be content, as the opening lines of his epic remind us, to be the English Virgil without feeling the compulsive drive to overgo Virgil, though that impulse, to judge from Ben Jonson's eulogy of Shakespeare, was not very far away even then. In such a spirit of literary chauvinism, Spenser cites "Dan Chaucer, well of English undefyled" and "pure well head of poesie" (*FQ*, IV.ii.32; VII.vii.9) as his chief poetic precursor, when the influences of Ariosto and Tasso are actually far more pervasive.[11] Of course even Ariosto and Tasso can be seen as Spenser's natural models, since they too were engaged in the attempt to create a vernacular epic of "fine fabling," in Bishop Hurd's phrase, to equal the "good sense" and regularity of the classics.

This paucity of native models doubtless made for a freedom to absorb influences that might account for Spenser's apparently carefree eclecticism of language and form as op-

---

[11] See A. Bartlett Giamatti, *Play of Double Senses: Spenser's* Faerie Queene (Englewood Cliffs, 1975), pp. 28-40, 47-52; and Alice S. Miskimin, *The Renaissance Chaucer* (New Haven, 1975), pp. 35-70. The latter, though concerned to establish a kind of Chaucerian influence on Spenser, accurately points out that "When such a poet calls strong attention to his historical perspective and asserts relationship, it is worthwhile to try to be aware both of what he wants to acknowledge, and of what he may omit. . . . Spenser's allusions to Chaucer are, I think, fascinating because they pay homage and seem to define relatedness which reading of the poems does not confirm." p. 44.

The Poetics of Modernity

posed to Milton's austere homogeneity. Yet when we turn from the poetic situation to the poetic practice of each, we see that even Spenser wholly reinvents the models he adopts, his Chaucer as well as his Ariosto and Virgil, although more quietly and unobtrusively than Milton. The "Mutabilitie Cantos" are by no means a simple repetition of *The Parliament of Fowls*, just as Spenser's archaizing language is not Chaucer's. For once a model or tradition is chosen, whether in an atmosphere of freedom or constraint, both the earlier and later poet—unless he is content merely to be a translator, and the Elizabethans produced many—face the same problem of creatively and coherently renovating his models. This Milton does to Virgil, Spenser to Ariosto and Chaucer, Chaucer to Boccaccio and Dante, as any poet who remains of more than antiquarian interest must. And if literary history is to represent the poet's achievement in its distinctiveness, it is the poetic uses to which he puts his models rather than the poetic situation he shares with his contemporaries that must be addressed.

There are instructive paradoxes here that bear directly on our reconsideration of literary history and influence. Milton deliberately chooses one poetic mode as opposed to another and, having chosen, rhetorically disowns and poetically revises it. Spenser chooses several poetic modes, and, having chosen, rhetorically privileges the least pervasive of them while poetically renovating them all. Most concepts of literary influence, including the most recent ones, do not take account of these deliberate indirections and contradictions, because they take their cue from the word "influence" and present it as an essentially passive and involuntary process of being filled or controlled from without, like being called to the church or coming down with "flu." Yet in Milton's case, the flow between past and poet is clearly two-way, resulting in the paradox that he simultaneously permits himself to be influenced and disclaims being influenced. And in Spenser's case too, a certain willfulness makes itself felt in so far as he repeatedly claims, for his own purposes, to

Homer and Others

have been profoundly influenced by a poet who is among the least palpable of his influences. No theory of literary history can afford to ignore this willful, in Milton's case positively aggressive, constituent in the modernity of every literary era. When it is neglected, as it is in most evolutionary theories dominated by romantic metaphors of organicism, literary history becomes too quiet. There is continuity but little interaction between works, between poets, or between periods. For the stages of an organism's growth or a species' evolution, though dependent on earlier phases of development, are necessarily discrete from them, as butterflies are from caterpillars or men are from apes. The process of change in the arts becomes deceptively serene and orderly, as deceptively serene as the peaceful transfer of power in modern democracies, or the apostolic succession.

An example from the historiography of Elizabethan drama will illustrate the point. From the time of its resurrection at the hands of romantic antiquarians through the early decades of this century, the Elizabethan drama had serious violence done to it by a critical and theatrical approach that expected from it and sought to find in it the conventions of nineteenth-century stage naturalism. Lamb believed that *King Lear* was unstageable, as did Bradley; Coleridge was preoccupied with Iago's motivation or the absence thereof; Bradley faults Shakespeare's construction for its fourth-act slackening of tension—as if Shakespeare composed in terms of a five-act structure. By the nineteen thirties and forties, it was becoming clear through the work of Stoll, Schücking, and others, that much of what had seemed faulty or perplexing in Elizabethan drama could be made sense of by studying the medieval and pre-Shakespearean drama and recognizing the persistence of those conventions on the popular Elizabethan stage. It is by now a critical commonplace that many of the characteristic features of Elizabethan drama are inherited from late medieval conventions of characterization, plot-structure, and subject-matter. Indeed, we are all used to saying that Shakespeare

The Poetics of Modernity

and his contemporaries cannot be fully understood without knowledge of them. Yet a curious ambivalence within the scholarship that has brought us to this point (and without which the present book could not be written) remains unresolved. On the one hand, we are quick to point to the underlying continuity between late medieval and Elizabethan drama; on the other, we are equally quick to dismiss the crudeness, naiveté, and archaism of medieval plays and assert the superior mimetic quality of the Elizabethans. In one breath, we claim that medieval conventions are fundamental and determining forces on Shakespeare, and, in the next, disclaim them as "fossils," "vestiges," and "survivals" of an outdated technique within the increasing naturalism of Shakespeare and his major contemporaries. In most accounts, and often in the same account, these medieval elements are regarded as at once fundamental and outmoded, essential yet expendable. The co-existence of medieval and "modern" elements, and the relationship between them, within an Elizabethan play cannot be satisfactorily explained by recourse to the evolutionary model that literary historians have widely adopted.

By contrast, most revolutionary theories of literary history are too noisy. Their plots of tradition and revolt offer plenty of interaction between works, between poets, and between periods, but little continuity. They tend to become a record of fits and starts, of impossibly quiescent reigns and impossibly spontaneous outbursts. Here we have convention, there revolt; here medieval, there renaissance, men; here classics, there romantics; here romantics, there moderns. We may come to feel that literary history can only turn into such a schismatic and spasmodic affair when it becomes a history of poetic manifestoes rather than poetic practice. Its nearest analogues and dominant metaphors are from military or political history, those histories of battles that changed the world, or perhaps of Latin American republics. This revolutionary model of an *avant-garde* seeking to overthrow traditional, later to be equated with bourgeois, forms might well seem closer than the evolutionary model to the pronouncements of the poets themselves, particularly though again not exclusively of later poets. Baudelaire refers, not unironically, to "the fighting poets," and Keats sees literary history since the Renaissance as a "grand march of intellect."[12]

The Elizabethan drama has often been thus regarded, as bursting out of the bondage of medieval and Tudor forms on the strength of the nationalism arising from the defeat of the Armada, and led by the revolutionary figures of Kyd and Marlowe. Marlowe in particular offers a focus for such a view—he is styled by one scholar "a fellow traveller with all the subversive currents of his age."[13] Indeed, we have only to recall the self-proclaimed repudiation of the "jigging vein of rhyming mother wits" in favor of "the stately tent of war" of the prologue to *Tamburlaine* to realize the extent to which the military model of literary change is suggested by the play itself. There, the hapless Bajazeth may be seen as the chief representative within the play of a long line of ranting oriental tyrants extending backward from Preston's Cambyses to the Biblical Herods and Pharoahs and allegorical Rex Vivus and Rex Mundus of medieval drama. In having his fuller-throated and more effective hero defeat Bajazeth, bend his precursor in worlddominion into his "footstool," Marlowe might well seem to be commenting on his own poetic achievement, and to have made good the opening boast of his prologue to create a new and revolutionary kind of drama. The military and political history enacted *in* the play may be read as a metaphor for the literary history enacted *by* the play.

Such a revolutionary view of literary history seems to arise quite naturally, in fact, from the subject-matter of military conflict and triumph that dominates earlier epic tradition. From the point of view of Augustan Rome, it might well

---

12 *Ecrits intimes* (Editions de la Pleiade, Paris, 1930), p. 194; To John Hamilton Reynolds, May 3, 1818 in *The Letters of John Keats*, ed. Maurice Buxton Forman (Oxford, 1952), p. 143.
13 Harry Levin, *The Overreacher* (Cambridge, Mass., 1952), p. 2.

seem that "*Graecia capta ferum victorem cepit,*" in Horace's words, "*et artes intulit agresti Latio.*" The prestige of the Homeric epic, with its vision of a heroism essentially individualistic or at most tribal, would thus have to be overthrown for a truly Roman epic, celebrating a new form of heroism that observes the reconciliatory demands of an imperial order, to emerge. It is precisely the older Achillean heroism that is defeated and superseded within the *Aeneid* when Aeneas defeats Turnus to assure future Roman glory. *Dios* Achilles and *polytropos* Odysseus give place to a new type of hero, *pius* Aeneas. Yet from Milton's viewpoint—"with this over and above, of being a Christian"[14]—the heroic mode of all classical epic must seem "erring," a fitter example for Satan than for Adam or Christ, through whom "the better fortitude / Of patience and heroic martyrdom" can now be triumphantly sung. Even when the overtly military subject-matter of the epic is abandoned, a similar strategy of reaction can be seen to operate, the abandonment of the public world of arms and the hero being part of that strategy. Wordsworth, for example, defines the form and argument of his own projected epic of "the individual mind" in respectful antagonism toward Milton. The success of his strategy is evident in Keats' remark that Milton "did not think into the human heart, as Wordsworth has done."[15] We may begin to suspect that the romantic idealization of the Renaissance and the classics into the "pure serene" Keats sought and found in Chapman's Homer is itself part of a campaign to open up new imaginative realms, the "untrodden region" of subjectivity of Keats' "Ode to Psyche." Milton and the other renaissance giants, that is, could be faulted and overcome precisely in their apparently untroubled sublimity, turning the domain of public poetry over which they had ruled once again into public domain.

[14] *The Student's Milton*, p. 525. Milton's transformation of epic conventions and the transvaluation of classical heroism it entails is treated by John Steadman, *Milton and the Renaissance Hero* (Oxford, 1957).
[15] *The Letters of John Keats*, p. 143.

Homer and Others

It should be recognized, however, that this military view of literary history, in which the poet is seen as a young champion who engages the giants of the past at what he takes to be their Achilles' heels and liberates the realm of poetry from their sway, only reverses the terms of the serene genetic historicism already discussed without really moving beyond them.[16] The concept of "tradition" has always carried with it the more sinister and military sense of "betrayal" and can be seen as something that does not necessarily nourish and sustain the individual talent but must be betrayed by the individual talent if he is to distinguish himself and not be betrayed by it. It is thus not surprising that modern literary history has increasingly come to be regarded as being led by an *avant-garde* perennially alert for opportunities to betray, by turning against, their rearward commanders. But it should also be clear by now that even if this revolutionary view is closer to that promulgated by poets themselves, or by some poets, than its evolutionary counterpart, it is itself only an enabling myth for the poets who employ it, a precondition or pretext for the production of their own art. Their creative act, however, is demonstrably more complex than is suggested by a view of literary history that would describe that act in terms of the sneer of a conquering hero or the defiance of an Oedipal son. Poetry "is not," as Claudio Guillén has written, "composed by unambitious writers in a peaceful universe where the greatest of literary accomplishments are freely and justly made available to the proper audience of enlightened men";[17] that is to say, poetry is not

---

[16] This is apparent, for example, in Baudelaire's reflection on "the fighting poets" cited above:

A ajouter aux métaphores militaires:
Les poètes de combat.
Les littérateurs d'avant-garde.

Ces habitudes de métaphores militaires dénotent des esprits, non pas militants, mais faits pour la discipline, c'est-à-dire pour la conformité, des esprits nés domestiques, des esprits belges, qui ne peuvent penser qu'en société.

[17] *Literature as System* (Princeton, 1971), p. 46.

The Poetics of Modernity

without its own politics and propaganda. But neither can it be reduced to internecine warfare.

The fact is that neither the evolutionary nor the revolutionary model of literary history is adequate to describe the complex relation between the poet and his past that obtains within actual poems. Even so militant a poet as Marlowe seems to acknowledge within his own work that in poetry, unlike war, his precursors can be captured but cannot really be done away with. In *Tamburlaine*, for example, the vehemence of its opening disavowal of tradition has the ring of a Freudian *Verneinung*, a denial that by protesting too much affirms the presence of that which is denied. It is only because Tamburlaine still retains an inescapable resemblance to Bajazeth and his fellow ranting tyrants that his distinctive wit and potency, his ability to turn his own not wholly unconventional language into action, is defined by contrast. Similarly, it is only because Marlowe retains his dramatic tradition in an internalized or sublated form, however roughly he deals with it within his work, that his own advance upon that tradition can begin to appear. The play's relation to its tradition becomes one of disjuncture and dependence, discontinuity and continuity, at the same time.

Marlowe's plays, while claiming a revolutionary victory, thus bring in the *ancien regime* through the back door. His blatant departures from medieval conventions—the refusal to punish the blasphemous and tyrannical Tamburlaine after the manner of *de casibus* "tragedy," or to have Faustus repent as countless morality protagonists had done before him—each departure from tradition also re-affirms the vital persistence of tradition. For these "departures" are finally only a borrowing and re-arranging of terms provided by tradition. (This is of course not to endorse an evolutionary view of Marlowe, since the persistence of medieval dramatic convention within his work is hardly "vestigial," but vital and necessary.) A similarly complex relation between poem and prototype occurs within the epics we have glanced at. Aeneas re-enacts the ruthless heroism of Achilles and Turnus in the very act of distinguishing himself from them. Christ performs his own *aristeia,* not altogether unlike that of the Homeric heroes he supersedes, in putting down Satan's rebellion in book six of *Paradise Lost.* What is still needed is a general theory of literary history and influence that accounts at once for the continuously subversive and radically conservative character of literature as it moves through time, that allows for both interaction and continuity between works, between poets, between periods, and between national literatures. Obviously, not all these relations will be within the reach of the present study.

In the ambivalence with which Milton sublates the classical epic and Marlowe the medieval drama within their own work, however, we do have the basis for such a theory. If these examples are not wholly unrepresentative, literature seems to carry its own history encoded or inscribed within it. It might be possible, then, to derive literary history from within literature itself rather than impose upon it an historical model drawn from the apparently non-literary contexts of the natural organic world, or political and military history, or the sublimated savagery of the Freudian family romance.[18] In the instances of Marlowe and Milton, the versions of the literary past included within their work are quite clearly *sub*versions, are explicitly offered, that is, to subvert or disestablish the traditions within which their work exists. Of course not all poets are temperamentally so self-righteous or self-advertising, or so openly contemptuous of their predecessors, as Milton or Marlowe, but that means only that the subversions of tradition within their work will be less explicit and showy and the literary historian's work of recognizing and reconstructing them more delicate.

At the same time, Marlowe's subversion of native dramatic

---

[18] Bloom's Freudian model of strong fathers and weak sons combines the organic or genetic continuity of the natural model with the embattled discontinuity of the military model. It retains, that is, the distorting element of each while remaining no less extrinsic to the literature it describes.

The Poetics of Modernity

tradition is quite obviously a perversion or parody of it, a twisting of it to fit his own purposes. A judicious study of the medieval drama would no doubt find those plays far less contemptible than Marlowe's or even Shakespeare's aspersions—"It out-herods Herod"—suggest. As Dante distinguishes between "the allegory of poets" and "the allegory of theologians," we must distinguish between the literary history of poets, which tends to be too polemical, and the literary history of professors, which tends to be too tranquil. For Marlowe and Shakespeare are primarily concerned not to be judicious in their treatment of those old plays but to write their own, which necessitates their disdaining them to some degree. In the case of Marlowe, a classically trained poet, his choice after *Dido* to work in a native rather than neoclassical mode may have a lot to do with the relative contemptibility, the potential for contemptuous distortion, those old plays allowed. (Elizabethan scholars, not unlike romanticists, often take their cue from the poets they study and adopt the attitude of their subjects toward the past without knowing it; that is, they take Marlowe's or Shakespeare's subversions and perversions of the medieval drama for the thing itself.) Yet it should be obvious that the poet's version of his literary past has no real existence outside his work. Marlowe's medieval drama is no more the medieval drama than Milton's Virgil is Virgil or Virgil's Homer, Homer. Otherwise we could not account for the fact that the *Odyssey* does not strike us as a wide-eyed adventure story, nor the *Iliad* as a callous glorification of war, while we read them, even if we read them after the *Aeneid*, which implicitly represents them as such to create by internal contrast its own more ironic and melancholy vision of *lacrimae rerum*.

The example of Homer provides an opportunity to dispel two superstitions, which we have addressed only obliquely up to this point and which still spook our attempts to write genuinely literary literary history: one psychological or biographical, and the other chronological or historical. The psychological fallacy holds that the impulse to distinguish himself which moves a poet to distort prior works into foils for his own operates only or mainly in those poets of a particularly self-assertive cast of mind, like Marlowe or Milton or their romantic followers. The chronological fallacy, that this impulse to self-distinction operates only or mainly in later, more crowded and competitive, periods, even if we obligingly backdate our notion of a later period to include the Renaissance. The two notions are logically and chronologically related. The expressive theory of poetry (and concomitant interest in the biography and psychology of the poet) originate in Europe at the same time as does the nostalgic myth of a noble and un-self-conscious folk poetry lost with the coming of civilization, which is to say, with the Eighteenth Century. It is not difficult to see how the two notions would sustain one another. But if it can be shown that Homer, at once the most elusive and anonymous of European poets, as the perennial "Homeric question" confirms, and the proverbial "dawn poet"—for Schiller the type of the "naive" poet untrammeled by the complexity and self-consciousness of modern civilization; for Keats, the poet "standing aloof in giant ignorance"—if it can be shown that Homer works by a process of sublation and subversion analogous to that of Marlowe or Milton or the romantics, then both notions are simultaneously laid to rest. The process of sublation becomes a function of literature proper and not a reflex of history or psychology.

The task is lightened somewhat by the work of Parry and Lord, who have established, if nothing else that the author(s) of the *Iliad* and *Odyssey* did not stand aloof or alone but somewhere toward the end of a long and fecund tradition of heroic song. The bard Demodocus in Book VIII of the *Odyssey* may be taken as representative of that tradition. Demodocus is like Homer, to be sure—he is blind; he has encoded within him all "the ways of life," presumably can sing songs of triumph and defeat, *Odysseys* and *Iliads*; and he sings of divine adultery and altercations. But in some ways he is more like the bards who must have preceded and

The Poetics of Modernity

surrounded Homer, in so far as his songs are episodic and fragmentary. One of his performances, the one I want to focus on, may even correspond to an actual epic entitled *The Sack of Troy*, the outline of which is preserved among Proclus' synopses of the Epic Cycle:[19]

> The minstrel stirred, murmuring to the god, and soon
> clear words and notes came one by one, a vision
> of the Akhaians in their graceful ships
> drawing away from shore: the torches flung
> and shelters flaring: Argive soldiers crouched
> in the close dark around Odysseus: and
> the horse, tall on the assembly ground of Troy.
> For when the Trojans pulled it in, themselves,
> up to the citadel, they sat nearby
> with long-drawn-out and hapless argument....
> For Troy must perish, as ordained, that day
> she harbored the great horse of timber; hidden
> the flower of Akhaia lay, and bore
> slaughter and death upon the men of Troy.
> He sang, then, of the town sacked by Akhaians
> pouring down from the horse's hollow cave,
> this way and that way raping the steep city,
> and how Odysseus came like Ares to
> the door of Deiphobos, with Menelaos,
> and braved the desperate fight there—
> conquering once more by Athena's power.
> The splendid minstrel sang it.
>
> (VIII, 499-525)

It is not that the song Demodocus sings of Odysseus' triumphant stratagem, the wooden horse and fall of Troy, is badly sung; we are told it is beautifully sung. But like

[19] See *Hesiod: The Homeric Hymns and Homerica*, ed. Hugh G. Evelyn-White (Loeb Classical Library, Cambridge, Mass., 1943), pp. xxx-xxxiii. Quotations from Homer are from *The Odyssey*, trans. Robert Fitzgerald (New York, 1961), and *The Iliad*, trans. Richmond Lattimore (Chicago, 1951).

everything else in Phaeacia, it is too beautiful, too harmonious, too composed—in sum, too artful to be true.

Much as the lifeless serenity depicted on the Grecian urn serves as a deliberate and necessary foil to set off the "breathing human passion" of Keats' ode, so Demodocus' disturbingly painless song of war serves a similar function within Homer's poem. This becomes clearer if we consider the immediate narrative and dramatic context of the song:

> And Odysseus
> let the bright molten tears run down his cheeks,
> weeping the way a wife mourns for her lord
> on the lost field where he has gone down fighting
> the day of wrath that came upon his children.
> At sight of the man panting and dying there,
> she slips down to enfold him, crying out;
> then feels the spears, prodding her back and shoulders,
> and goes bound into slavery and grief.
> Piteous weeping wears away her cheeks;
> but no more piteous than Odysseus' tears,
> cloaked as they were, now, from the company.
> (VIII, 525-536)

Odysseus weeps, it is fair to say, not over Demodocus' glittering song—there is nothing there for a Greek to cry about—but over all that has been left out of the song, the shadowing now supplied by Homer. That shadowing takes the form of the simile following hard upon Demodocus' song, in which Homer returns us to the scene of battle from the new and painful viewpoint of the victim, in which the suffering of the victim *and that of the victor* are explicitly equated. The extent of that suffering in exile forms the subject-matter of the next three books, narrated by Odysseus not simply in response to Alcinous' inquiries about him but in contradiction of Demodocus' idealization of him as "a legend in his own time." Homer brings us a long way from Demodocus' song of total and painless triumph and as close to what Virgil will term (in a passage modelled di-

The Poetics of Modernity

rectly on this one) "the tears of things" as Homer ever approaches.

For the Phaeacian minstrel and king the fall of Troy is *only a story*; they have long ago succumbed to what Henry James calls "the coercive charm of form":

> Tell me why you should grieve so terribly
> over the Argives and the fall of Troy.
> That was all gods' work, weaving ruin there
> so it should make a song for men to come!
> (VIII, 579-582)

"*Tout, au monde, existe pour aboutir à un livre*"[20]—Alcinous is the Mallarmé of the epic. It is only fitting that Homer presents the eventual fate of Phaeacia, that place where all is artful and ceremonious, in an image of literal reification. Phaeacia exists in order to end up landlocked, bound by stone sculpture—the antithesis of Odysseus' and the poem's kinship with that world of organic process evoked in such master-images as Odysseus' hunting scar, his great wooden bow, and his bed of living olive-wood. Odysseus rejects a Phaeacian form of idyllic stasis each time it is offered. The only answer Odysseus could make to Alcinous' question, why he should grieve so over the fall of Troy, is that the Trojan war did take place, that he was there—*ipse miserima vidi, / et quorum pars magna fui*—and he makes it in the form of his own story. Homer is to Demodocus as Virgil is to Homer; Homer fills in, that is, all that pain which in Demodocus' version has been elided or neutralized or sublimated by and into art. Or almost all that pain, since it remains for Virgil to rewrite Demodocus' story of the sack of Troy in something like the fullness of its pathos in Book II of the *Aeneid*. Although Alcinous recognizes the primacy of the sign ("so it should make a song for men to come"), he and his minstrel ignore the arbitrariness and deceptive-

[20] Stephane Mallarmé, "Le Livre, Instrument Spirituel" in *Oeuvres Complètes*, ed. Henri Mondor et G. Jean-Aubry (Edition Pleiade, Paris, 1963), p. 378.

ness of the sign. They remain critically unaware of the ontological discrepancy between any sign system and what it signifies, between the forms of poetry and the life that those forms mediate. It is through his consciousness of this fatal gap that Homer is able to narrow (though never close) it, to present something more like the truth and totality of Odysseus' experience than anything the historical Demodokoi before him ever dreamed. There is an important sense in which the earlier mimetic poet, who seems so conservative, like Homer or Shakespeare, is more daring in his attempt to bridge the gap between sign and significance than the later symbolist poet, who proclaims his innovativeness like Mallarmé or Rilke. The former begins where the latter ends—on the far side of that gap—and his work becomes a quietly heroic, though necessarily unfulfilled, mission of recrossing it.

Homeric epic depends on the relative thinness and partiality of its inscribed tradition in order to create by internal contrast its own illusion of density and fullness. What once seemed to classical scholars like digressions or interpolations, the "fossils" of older stories that had somehow found a resting place in Homer, become on closer scrutiny the condition of Homer's integrity and originality. Such stories-within-the story as Demodocus' light epyllion of Ares' seduction of Aphrodite and punishment by Hephaestus, or Menelaus' romantic travelogue of shipwreck and deliverance in Egypt, or the reiterated cautionary tale of Agamemnon's tragic homecoming at the hands of Clytemnestra, or even the embryonic *Bildungsroman* of the "Telemachia" are cartoons of the story of Odysseus and Penelope, partial models or photographic negatives or rough sketches of the *Odyssey* itself. All have their own poetic and generic integrity and almost certainly their own traditions as independent stories, but all are employed in the *Odyssey* as analogous, though finally inadequate or inapplicable, versions of Odysseus' more intractable, less conventional experience. Although this is not the place to discuss each of these instances in detail, I would suggest that they work together to build up a forestructure of meaning and expectation that the poem goes on to contradict at least as much as confirm.

Although the *Iliad* contains moments comparable in effect to that of Demodocus' song—our glimpse of Helen weaving the war into a tapestry, or the description of Achilles' shield —it presents no bard in action or song-within-the-song as such. Yet it is no less informed by recollections—I categorically refuse to call them "fossils"—of a poetic past. The "Dolonea," for example, that interlude of guile within a poem of force, is a quiet and small-scale prefiguration of the taking of Troy; the prototypical "catalogue of ships," a form of dictionary of national biography (very possibly adapted by Homer from Boiotian epic[21]) that fails, like all biographical dictionaries or obituaries, to catch and fix the heroic essence of the lives it records, something the *Iliad* will do more successfully. More resonant within the *Iliad* as a whole is the famous episode in Book IX that might be entitled the "Meleagrid." There, Achilles' old tutor, Phoenix, recalls the story of another angry hero and another siege, a story that some pre-Homeric bard must once have sung:[22]

[21] See the introduction to *Hesiod: The Works and Days, The Theogony, and The Shield of Achilles*, trans. Richmond Lattimore (Ann Arbor, 1959).

[22] Meleager is mentioned by Aristotle (*Poetics*, XIII) as a subject of tragedy and is frequently depicted in classical art. On the mythological variations of the Meleager story, see J. T. Kakridis, *Homeric Researches* (Lund, 1949), pp. 11-64, and M. M. Willcock, "Mythological Paradeigma in the *Iliad*," *Classical Quarterly*, New Series, XIV (1964), 141-154. The Homeric passage in which his story is told was in antiquity and continues to be a focus of commentary. Denys Page, *History and the Homeric Iliad* (Berkeley, 1959), pp. 297-315, argues on the grounds of its differences of vocabulary and inconsistencies of detail that Phoenix' tale of Meleager must be a late addition to the *Iliad*. Though directly relevant to the question of Homeric authorship, his argument does not affect my own, since Meleager's experience remains a significant and defining foil to Achilles', whenever and by whomever it was composed. Without it the *Iliad* would be a different

Homer and Others

> Thus it was in the old days also, the deeds that we hear of
> from the great men, when the swelling anger descended upon them.
> The heroes would take gifts; they would listen, and be persuaded.
> For I remember this action of old, it is not a new thing,
> And how it went; you are all my friends, I will tell it among you.
>
> (IX, 524-528)

Phoenix's tale presents an almost perfect model of Achilles' present situation and of the action of the *Iliad*. The hero, Meleager, has withdrawn in wrath from the war raging between the Couretes and his people, the Aetolians. When the Aetolian city of Calydon is on the verge of falling, the Aetolian elders, Meleager's mother and sisters, his dearest friends, and finally his bride entreat him in turn to drive back the Couretes' assault. After repeated refusals, Meleager relents in the nick of time, girds himself, "and drove back the day of evil from the Aetolians." To Phoenix it is a foregone conclusion that Achilles' problem is now solved by this appeal to heroic precedent, and he closes his story by warning Achilles not to be done out of the gifts promised him as Meleager had been. Of course Achilles' problem is not solved and he does not relent, at least not yet. Again Homer leads us to the edge of the ontological gap between sign and significance. No tale of anger and reconciliation from the past, no received form of myth-history, can suffice unto the day. In having Achilles reject the example of Meleager as a model for himself, Homer is also pointing out the inadequacy of one more received form to his own poetic task.

Just as Achilles defines himself *against* Meleager, so the *Iliad* defines itself *against* the "Meleagrid." For the two

---

and a lesser poem. Page's argument, if valid, does not bear on the artistic intent of the collective authorial consciousness we name "Homer."

stories are alike in so far as they are both tales of heroic alienation and reconciliation; yet they are unlike in so far as the alienation and reconciliation presented in the *Iliad* transcend that presented in Phoenix' tale by precisely the lengths to which Achilles holds out beyond Meleager, and the price which his reconciliation costs him beyond the material loss sustained by Meleager. Achilles, after all, eventually receives the gifts his prototype was denied. The poetic accrual is not simply a function of relative length. While greater length is a necessary condition of the *Iliad*'s superior realization, it is not a sufficient condition, for the *Iliad* could have been twice as long as it is and still not have significantly altered the form of the "Meleagrid." The difference proceeds from Homer's awareness, as opposed to Phoenix's or Demodocus' unawareness, that the language of poetry—of all poetry, not just classical poetry—is always a dead language in so far as it is a self-contained system operating by conventions of form that have no immediate connection with the human and living present.

As with form, so with the formula. This is not to suggest that Homer shared our modern view of language as system, but rather that he employs his own poetic language in a way wholly compatible with and interpretable within such a view. The late Adam Parry, for example, has cogently demonstrated that Achilles is unique within the *Iliad* in having no language in which to express his condition, the formulaic language of oral epic tradition being inadequate to express "the awful distance between appearance and reality; between what Achilles expected and what he got; between the truth that society imposes on men and what Achilles has seen to be true for himself."[23] Yet Achilles nonetheless manages to express his essential condition, but only "by misusing the language he disposes of. He asks questions that cannot be answered and makes demands that

[23] "The Language of Achilles," *The Language and Background of Homer*, ed. G. S. Kirk (Cambridge, 1964), pp. 48-54.

cannot be met. He uses conventional expressions where we least expect him to." Parry's conclusion is not only crucial to the meaning of the *Iliad* but suggestive of its significance within literary history: "Homer uses the epic speech a long poetic tradition gave him to transcend the limits of that speech."

What Parry does not go on to state is that the "conventional" usages of the heroic idiom by Sarpedon and others in the poem exist in a fundamental sense for the sake of Achilles' distortions of it. They make Achilles' enactment of his transcendent selfhood possible and recognizable. Whether or not the heroic formula had ever been skewed out of its pristine integrity before Achilles does it—here Parry accepts at face value Homer's pastoralization of the past and makes into a matter of literary history what must remain a matter of literary theory—Homer must pretend it had not been done before in order to tell Achilles' story. Like Achilles, the poet can only begin to say what he is about by saying what he is not about. And like Achilles, he can say it only through the dead grammar of previous poetry. But by shocking that grammar sufficiently, by twisting it into unprecedented postures, he can make it generate new and living forms, at least momentarily. These "original" formulae are discernible and decipherable as such, however, only because they exist within the work in juxtaposition with older ones. It becomes the labor of the literary historian to decipher those new forms from his knowledge of the old, as both appear within the weathered Rosetta stone that is every poem. In the case of the *Iliad*, Parry has made an exemplary start.

The fact that Homer's place within a putative history of the Greek epic can begin to appear, even in the absence of previous extant epics and solely from within his own work, is revealing in itself. It shifts the basis for our speculation on literary history, influence, and originality from the extraneous and arbitrarily privileged ground of chronology or psychology onto a purely textual ground. By beginning

The Poetics of Modernity

in the effort to decipher the arch hermeneutic the poet has practiced on his predecessors to create his own text in the first place and literary history at the same time, a new and overdue integration of literary history and interpretation becomes possible; and by refocusing attention on the traditionally mimetic and referential claim of literature, especially but not exclusively of earlier literature, an alternative to the dark and compulsive subjectivity of recent literary-historical speculation becomes available. Indeed, Bate and Bloom have said a great deal about what might be termed the pretextual aspect of literary history, the poet's concern with emergence and priority, the private anguish before past greatness that precedes poetic choices and acts and that Pope, writing about himself, projects onto Virgil:

> When first young Maro in his boundless mind
> A work to outlast immortal Rome designed,
> Perhaps he seemed above the critic's law,
> And but from Nature's fountains scorned to draw;
> But when to examine every part he came,
> Nature and Homer were, he found, the same.[24]

But they have so far said little about the textual issue of this timeless predicament, the revelation that nature and Homer may, in fact, not be the same. The poet is able to break the monopoly of the past on poetic representation by re-opening an appeal from poetry to nature and producing a text that by seeming, in its turn, identical with nature will tonguetie his followers. That the originality of a given work or the modernity of a given movement is an essentially mimetic, and only incidentally a temporal or psychological matter is implicit in the rallying-cries with which successive *avant-garde* poets and movements have announced themselves: "verisimilitude," "realism," "naturalism," "surrealism," even "symbolism" and "expressionism." All lay claim

---

[24] "An Essay on Criticism," ll. 130-135.

Homer and Others

not only to being new but to being true, or at least to approximating more closely than their predecessors a public, but hitherto unpublished, truth.

The study of literary history thus becomes inseparable from the study of mimesis. Their common point of departure is the very secondariness accorded to poetry in relation to "reality" by literary theorists from Plato and Aristotle through Coleridge and Auerbach, on which our conceptions of both literary history and mimesis have been based. Literary history is still viewed as the *shadow* of social or intellectual history, much as literature itself is viewed as a *reflection* or *imitation* of "reality." If the process of sublation described above plays a central role in a theory of literary history, it should also play a central role in a theory of mimesis, since the models which serve as historical points of departure also serve as mimetic points of reference within the work that includes them. The inherent secondariness of poetry and the poetic function remains, though not simply in relation to "reality" or "history" or "nature" or "experience" or "truth" or "life"—those largest and shiftiest of abstractions—but in relation to previous poetry, which in turn is also secondary. For the notion that poetry imitates "life" leads nowhere, in so far as we have no way of conceiving of, much less comprehending, life except through the mediation of sign-systems, however rudimentary, un-self-conscious, or popular—what Bacon called "idols" of the marketplace, tribe, and theater—that is to say, through the necessary aid of art, which is inescapable. Just as there is no unmediated vision, so is there no unmythologized life. Life as the referent of literature most certainly exists, but it cannot be known directly; it is simply "unavailable" to the perceiving mind without art, and remains in that sense dependent on it. It follows that art does not so much imitate life, as *mediate* life, and art in that special sense is always primary. What art does manifestly imitate is previous art or the artistic constituent of human life without which

The Poetics of Modernity

human life would be literally inconceivable and unimaginable. This is implied whenever we use the term "representation" as a synonym for mimesis, since there is no reason why life should have to be *re*presented if it could be presented directly. It is the mediating convention of presentation, which is art, that is presented again and again in continually altered forms. Moreover, "mirrors" as opposed to "lamps" are not at issue here, since both metaphors can be taken to mean either that the poem reveals a light and life separate from itself, be they located in the world or in the self or soul, or that the poem reveals a light and life that has no real existence apart from it. It is on the latter understanding that our theory of mimesis must proceed.

Poets have always known at some level that all they can directly imitate is prior art as a means of indirectly imitating or, more accurately, triangulating or referring to nature. Renaissance classicists, who considered themselves, incidentally, the *avant-garde* of their day, established the Horatian ideal of literary imitation that was thought for several centuries to be the means of doing precisely this. The young poet, following this program, imitates the classical poets who were supposed to have held a monopoly on the principles of imitating life, what Pope quite accurately calls "nature methodized." The theory in its neoclassical form is of course a series of more or less fanciful footnotes to Aristotle, but even in the *Poetics* Sophocles is repeatedly recommended above all others as classic in very nearly his own time to the apprentice dramatists who probably formed Aristotle's audience—as the model, the imitation of whom would lead closest to the imitation of nature itself. Not only in the classical and neoclassical drama, where the theory of mimesis originates and has centered, but in other modes and eras as well, every change in the conventions of verisimilitude is primarily a change in the literary precedents and canons chosen for imitation. When Wordsworth, for example, decides that the proper object of poetic imitation is "incidents and situations from common life

Homer and Others

... in a selection of language really used by men,"[25] he must find an imaginative correlative for those realities he would imitate in the folk tales and ballads he does imitate.

But the poetics of imitation harbor a further irony that provides the basis of the present study. Even its purest earlier exponents like Ben Jonson or Racine, both accomplished classicists, depart significantly from the Plautine and Euripidean models they profess to follow as the surest route to the imitation of nature. Not even the strict imitation of previous literature, it would seem, is possible for the true poet. Jonson, for example, asserts contradictorily in his *Discoveries* that the aspiring poet should imitate an ancient author "till he grow very Hee," but that the ancients are "guides not commanders,"[26] and Racine goes through similar gyrations in his prefaces to reconcile his conflicting claims to imitation and innovation. Horace, after all, had blithely or ironically counseled both. Although some might regard these self-contradictions as symptomatic of the "anxiety of influence," or would do so if they allowed the possibility of such anxiety before 1660, I submit rather that they reflect the autonomous logic of literature itself in so far as literature is *re*presentation.

How, then, has poetry been traditionally conceived of as an imitation at all when, strictly speaking, it imitates neither

---

[25] "Preface to the Second Edition of the 'Lyrical Ballads,' " *The Poetical Works of Wordsworth*, ed. Thomas Hutchinson (Oxford, 1932), p. 935. My account of the process by which literature imitates and is begotten by literature is to be distinguished from Northrop Frye's, as explicitly presented in his important essay "Nature and Homer," *Fables of Identity* (New York, 1963). In Frye's system, there is no room or allowance for change, since all works of a given genre are constituted by the same fundamental myths and archetypes, and myths and archetypes are by their very nature unchanging, recurrent, and eternally present. Milton's "Lycidas" is thus essentially the same poem as Bion's epitaph for Moschus. The impossibility of an historical poetics within such a system is self-evident, since the concept of priority, or even chronicity, is excluded from it.

[26] *Timber, or Discoveries*, pp. 638-639.

The Poetics of Modernity

nature nor previous poetry? The process of mimesis, I would suggest, is one of greater obliquity still and parallels the literary-historical process of sublation already described; it too is achieved, that is, by the deliberate misquotation or deformation of previous poetry within a given work. If the poet cannot be like Borges' Pierre Menard, who flawlessly recreates past works through relentless historical identification, he can at least be like Cervantes' Don Quixote, who creates a new form out of the shambles of an old by deliberately misapplying its conventions in an age too late. Cervantes invents the "realistic" novel not by including the windmills and barber's basins of "reality" in a narrative where they would previously have had no place—the fallacy that the novel achieves its characteristic realism by sheer inclusiveness or "thinginess" is still current—but by superimposing on them the forms of romance, giants and golden helmets, and showing that they do not fit. The giants and golden helmets of romance have in the process been demystified or made prosaic, but the windmills and barber's basins (not of "reality" but of the picaresque tale) have been remystified or made poetic. The Russian formalists would say "made strange." The effect of *ostranenie* or "defamiliarization" analyzed by Victor Shklovsky is not merely a device of realism peculiar to the novel, but the principle on which mimesis and literary history have always proceeded. To make it new the poet must make it strange, as Milton does the classical epic or Marlowe does the medieval drama or Homer the pre-Homeric heroic song. He simultaneously makes his own work true, or something more like "true." A given work thus openly uses or abuses a great deal of previous art only to create the illusion that it uses no art at all, that it presents the thing itself. From the point of view of the audience, every work becomes a *déjà vu*, or as Roland Barthes puts it in another context, a *déjà lu*, and simultaneously a *jamais vu* or *jamais lu*.

Our twin theories of literary history and mimesis have again converged. But lest either or both seem too positive, let me add this closing caveat. The very process by which

Homer and Others

poetry works its illusion of presence and plenitude and invites us to see and make connections between it and something outside it—the culture, mind, or life of the poet —also reminds us of its fictiveness and invalidates those connections. In his sublation of older poetry to make his own seem newer and truer by contrast, the poet cannot help but bring out the *likeness* that persists between his own work and his predecessors' even as he brings out their unlikeness. The poem which would appear new and true to the point of not being a poem at all becomes, by the very process that enables it to appear so, as potentially outmoded and factitious as the poem it mocks. Whatever vital continuity it would establish between itself and a referent outside itself is thus severed even as it is born. Poetry relapses into its own nature as fiction in the very instant it seems to transcend its fictionality. Just as the search for an historical starting-point for literary modernity will reveal, if rigorously pressed, only a more removed, ever receding, modernity, so the search for a mimetic reference for literature will turn up, not history, or reality, or experience, which remain forever missing and unavailable, but another convention of mimesis, like a play within a play or a mask beneath a mask. Poetry continually tells us, with Tennyson's Ulysses, that "all experience is an arch wherethro' / Gleams that untravell'd world whose margin fades / For ever and for ever when I move." If literature can never catch up and join with history, then its own history can never be captured by the literary form of historiography, no matter how it is reconstructed. This is not quite a counsel of despair, however, since the ultimate inauthenticity of any literary-historical model as history does not deny to it that provisional authenticity of literature which arises precisely as a function of its openly and self-consciously acknowledging its own fictionality. The following essays toward an historical poetics of Elizabethan tragedy, though admittedly not a literal, complete, or "true" history, do attempt to participate in this latter mode of knowledge.

CHAPTER 2

O'erdoing Termagant:
Hamlet

> That was the old way, Gossip, when Iniquity came in like Hokos Pokos, in a Juglers jerkin, with false skirts, like the Knave of Clubs! but now they are attir'd like men and women o' the time, the Vices, male and female!
> Ben Jonson, *The Staple of News*,
> 2nd Intermean, 14-17.

THERE is probably no more promising point of departure for the study of Shakespeare's relation to his dramatic past than Hamlet's advice to the players:

> O, it offends me to the soul to hear a robustious periwig-pated fellow tear a passion to tatters, to very rags, to split the ears of the groundlings, who (for the most part) are capable of nothing but inexplicable dumb shows and noise. I would have such a fellow whipp'd for o'erdoing Termagant. It out-herods Herod. Pray you avoid it. . . . Be not too tame neither; but let your own discretion be your tutor. Suit the action to the word, the word to the action; with this special observance, that you o'erstep not the modesty of nature: for anything so overdone is from the purpose of playing, whose end, both at the first and now, was and is, to hold, as 'twere, the mirror up to nature; to show virtue her own feature, scorn her own image, and the very age and body of the time his form and pressure.
>
> (III.ii.7-25)[1]

[1] All quotations of Shakespeare in my text are from *The Complete Pelican Shakespeare*, ed. Alfred Harbage (Baltimore, 1972).

Hamlet

At first glance, the speech seems perfectly straightforward and unambiguous. It begins with some practical pointers on acting and builds toward a general statement of the function of drama—one we would all readily agree with and quote often enough—which supports, in turn, the practical pointers. It evokes through many details an august tradition of classical and renaissance dramatic theory, and would seem to promote the kind of "modern" and "lifelike" drama we associate with Shakespeare at the expense of the old-fashioned and exaggerated drama we associate, often as a result of this speech, with the medieval stage. After all, Hamlet's discourse on the art of theater is, we like to say, the closest thing we have to a statement of Shakespeare's own aims and principles as a dramatist. Yet whether or not Hamlet's account of the purpose of playing is also Shakespeare's, the fact that it occupies a central place within the most theatrically self-conscious and complex of his plays makes it more problematic than is usually supposed, a text in certain respects ambiguous in its statement and inconsistent with the play that forms its context.

It is with the general statement of the function of drama that I am chiefly concerned here, both in its immediate application to *Hamlet* itself and in its wider implications for Shakespeare's work as a whole. In Hamlet's classic restatement of the commonplace—"to hold, as 'twere, the mirror up to nature"—the purpose of playing is twofold. Drama projects, on the one hand, a moral vision—"to show virtue her own feature, scorn her own image"—and on the other, a lifelike illusion—"the very age and body of the time his form and pressure." What Hamlet has done, in effect, is to conflate under the blanket phrase, "to hold the mirror up to nature," two distinct notions of drama, each with a long tradition and each in some degree antagonistic to the other in aim and method. The former, the view of the play as moral vision, transcends by its very nature considerations of time and place, associates drama with theology or moral philosophy, and is identifiable in Hamlet's account with medieval and Tudor allegorical theater—note the vestiges of personification in the phrases, "virtue *her own feature,* scorn *her own image."* The latter, the view of the play as lifelike illusion, is by its very nature time-bound and localized, associates drama with historiography, and is identifiable in Hamlet's account with the more or less naturalistic theater of classical Rome and renaissance Italy. Taken as a whole, Hamlet's speech is predominantly a plea for the new doctrine of dramatic illusionism and falls into line with the special pleading of such Elizabethan classicists as Sidney and Jonson. From such a point of view, to do Termagant at all is to overdo Termagant, for such roles as Termagant and Herod are written out of a homiletic rather than mimetic conception of drama, no matter how they were actually performed, in so far as they are offered as timeless and cautionary embodiments of wickedness and tyranny rather than as characterizations of human similitude. Moral images are not necessarily lifelike ones. But even though Hamlet's advice to the players stresses neoclassical decorum, the medieval conception of drama as a timeless moral vision, for all its apparent incompatibility, survives in it, as it does in the play of *Hamlet* itself.

For a specimen of that older dramatic mode we need look no further than the play-within-the-play. Hamlet describes it to Claudius as "the image of a murder done in Vienna: Gonzago is the duke's name; his wife, Baptista" (III.ii.247-249); he stresses, that is, the play's naturalistic representation of an historical event enacted in a specific place by specific people. Any resemblance to persons living or dead in the Danish court, he implies, is purely coincidental. But this description of *The Murder of Gonzago* does not correspond to the play we see. Its alternative title *The Mousetrap,* which Hamlet calls it "tropically" or figuratively, is really much more accurate, for the play is "tropical" or figurative in its very conception, a piece of mirror-literature in the older sense, and might have been called *A Looking-Glass for Elsinore and Denmark,* a dramatic *exemplum* reflecting the moral essence of many historical situations, pre-eminently the present state of Denmark and its recent past. *The Murder of Gonzago* represents, in sum, the first phase of a typical revenge action of what might be termed the first wave, of the kind produced during the late 1580's and early 1590's when the form was still explicitly involved with the Tudor morality drama and its clear-cut personifications of virtue and vice. It opens with the archaic device of a dumb-show, which presents, not at all inexplicably, the murder of an idealized king and husband and the seduction of his queen by the treacherous usurper, who in the logic of this convention would then have met his own nemesis in the form of a revenger, with order and justice restored.

Within the interrupted performance we see, the player-king and queen have shed all literal identity as Gonzago and Baptista; the emblematic garden in which the player-king lies down has replaced any more or less historical Vienna as the play's setting; and the debate on marital fidelity, delivered in stylistically archaic end-stopped couplets and balanced rhetorical figures, works to generalize and depersonalize the situation out of which they speak. The characters themselves are wholly idealized, perfect embodiments of faith in love expressing exemplary attitudes as they strive with each other in "gentilesse." By naturalistic canons, the lady protests too much and too archaically to be believed. For a moment it might seem as if we had somehow blundered into one of John Heywood's moral interludes, until the entrance of Lucianus makes the play's revenge-orientation quite clear. From Hamlet's remarks upon Lucianus' entrance—"Pox, leave thy damnable faces, and begin! Come, the croaking raven doth bellow for revenge" (III.ii.-264-265)—we can assume that the actor who plays Lucianus is indulging in a good deal of the Tudor equivalent of mustachio-twisting, exploiting the theatricality implicit in the Vice's role. Hamlet's line on "the croaking raven" is actually quoted from a speech in the pre-Shakespearean *True Tragedy of Richard III* (printed 1594) spoken by

O'erdoing Termagant

Richard just at the point when his own nemesis, Henry of Richmond, is close at hand.[2] The six lines that Lucianus, the counterpart of Richard in usurpation and seduction, has time to utter before Claudius, the counterpart of both within the world of *Hamlet*, breaks up the performance are in a vein familiar to students of those first-wave revenge plays—*The Spanish Tragedy, Soliman and Perseda, The True Tragedy of Richard III, Titus Andronicus*, and (dare I say it?) the *Ur-Hamlet*:

> Thoughts black, hands apt, drugs fit, and time agreeing;
> Confederate season, else no creature seeing;
> Thou mixture rank, of midnight weeds collected,
> With Hecate's ban thrice blasted, thrice infected,
> Thy natural magic and dire property
> On wholesome life usurp immediately.
>
> (III.ii.266-271)

At the very center of *Hamlet*, then, we have a substantial fragment of a primitive Elizabethan revenge tragedy, its morality affiliations—dumb-show, emblematic setting, generalizing rhetoric, virtue figures, and a highly theatrical Vice—intact. Like those older revenge plays and revenge-plays-within-revenge-plays on which it is modeled, *The Murder of Gonzago* is by Hamlet's own standards archaic, conventional, and anti-mimetic. Of its dramatic mode in general we might well conclude that in this style it is impossible to tell the truth.

It would be convenient to think that in moving with Hamlet from the banquet hall of the play scene to his mother's closet we have also moved forward through theatrical history, left behind an archaic theatricality with its stiff and stylized postures for contemporary realism with

---

[2] The actual lines (xviii, 1892-1893), which may help to explain Hamlet's impatience with this kind of drama, are worth quoting: "The screeking Raven sits croking for revenge. / Whole heads [sic] of beasts comes bellowing for revenge." *The True Tragedy of Richard the Third*, ed. W. W. Greg (Malone Society Reprints, Oxford, 1929), leaf Hv.

Hamlet

its more intimate disclosures of deepest personality, and thereby taken the measure of Shakespeare's enormous advance on naturalism in the decade since his own *Titus Andronicus*. The only trouble is that the closet scene is in certain respects not less archaic and anti-mimetic than the play scene, but more so. Despite its attractiveness to nineteenth-century characterological and twentieth-century psychoanalytic critics, the closet scene tells us little about Hamlet's alleged state of mind. For most of the scene he does not speak as a son to his mother at all, but as a preacher to a sinner, not out of personal feeling but out of impersonal *indignatio*. His language and the role it expresses work to generalize, depersonalize, and archaize the scene out of all recognition as a naturalistic rendering of a son's mixed feelings toward his mother:

> Such an act
> That blurs the grace and blush of modesty,
> Calls virtue hypocrite, and takes the rose
> From the fair forehead of an innocent love
> And sets a blister there, makes marriage vows
> As false as dicers' oaths. O, such a deed
> As from the body of contraction plucks
> The very soul, and sweet religion makes
> A rhapsody of words! Heaven's face doth glow,
> And this solidity and compound mass,
> With heated visage, as against the doom,
> Is thought-sick at the act.
>
> (III.iv.41-52)

No medieval preacher ever inveighed against the horrors of incest, its assault upon the entire fabric of God's consecrated order, with greater homiletic inspiration than Hamlet does here. No wonder T. S. Eliot, his neo-classicism at that stage of his career stronger than his neo-medievalism, could find no "objective correlative" within the play for Hamlet's speeches. Even Gertrude vaguely perceives that Hamlet's speech is inspired more by ancient texts than by

O'erdoing Termagant

any immediate situation: "Ay me, what act, / That roars so loud and thunders in the index?" (III.iv.51-52) Here, as in so much of the play, we are confronted not with the ravings of a disordered personality but with the heroic frenzy of the prophet's role.

Moreover, Gertrude's terms are theatrical as well as bookish. They recall Hamlet's own caveats to the players about mouthing lines, tearing a passion to tatters, and splitting the ears of the groundlings. Surely at this moment Hamlet o'erdoes Termagant and out-herods Herod, o'ersteps the modesty of nature, and violates his own neoclassical doctrines of decorum in speech and action as flagrantly as the most unreformed ham among the tragedians of the city. In sum, Hamlet turns the stage during the closet scene into something closely akin to the older *theatrum mundi* of Termagant and Herod, as he recasts the experience of the play into a straightforward morality drama in which everyone has a clear-cut and conventional role:

> What devil was't
> That thus hath cozened you at hoodman-blind?
> Eyes without feeling, feeeling without sight,
> Ears without hands or eyes, smelling sans all,
> Or but a sickly part of one true sense
> Could not so mope.
> Oh shame, where is thy blush? Rebellious hell,
> If thou canst mutine in a matron's bones,
> To flaming youth let virtue be as wax
> And melt in her own fire.
> (III.iv.77-86)

In Hamlet's rewriting of events, Gertrude is the misguided sinner related to the figure of hot-blooded youth, seduced by Vices like Will, Inclination, or Lust, in the moralities. Mary Magdalene, in the Digby play of that title, is a good example. Claudius is explicitly cast as such a Vice in Hamlet's morality, or rather as a composite Vice embodying several

Hamlet

sins—lust, drunkenness, riot, etc.—right down to the details of his costume in pre-Shakespearean stage-tradition:

> A vice of kings,
> A cutpurse of the empire and the rule,
> That from a shelf the precious diadem stole
> And put it in his pocket....
> A king of shreds and patches.
>
> (III.iv.99-103)

As for Hamlet himself, he takes on the role of a preacher, to be sure, specifically the chief virtue-figure of the morality, who tries to redeem the sinner from the snares of the Vice, usually, as Hamlet does here, by preaching him into repentance with Scriptural quotations and *exempla*, but often through a *coup de théâtre* like that of the two portraits of King Hamlet and Claudius, a device with many analogues in morality tradition. It recalls, for example, the picture of Wit in Redford's *Wit and Science* (c. 1531-47), which he no longer resembles after falling prey to the Vice, Idleness. When Wit incredulously looks into a glass held up by Reason, he finds himself all spotted and deformed. Gertrude's response to Hamlet's portrait-test underscores the parallel:

> Thou turn'st mine eyes into my very soul,
> And there I see such black and grained spots
> As will not leave their tinct.
>
> (III.iv.90-92)

Although Gertrude speaks figuratively here, her case had been literally represented on the medieval stage as far back as *Wisdom, Who Is Christ* (1461-85), where the fallen Anima "apperythe in the most horrybull wyse, fowlere than a fende" and is chastized into repentance by Wisdom: "Se howe ye have dysvyguryde yowr soule! / Beholde yowrselff; loke veryly in mynde!" (900-902).[3] Throughout the scene,

---

[3] *The Macro Plays*, ed. Mark Eccles (E.E.T.S., Oxford, 1969), p. 143.

O'erdoing Termagant

Hamlet holds the mirror up to nature in the same sense that a long line of preaching Virtues had done before him. "Forgive me this my virtue," he tells Gertrude, explicitly identifying himself with those older figures,

> For in the fatness of these pursy times
> Virtue itself of vice must pardon beg.
> Yea, curb and woo for leave to do him good.
> (III.iv.153-156)

His terms might be capitalized. Again they have the force and feel of personifications enacting a drama older than the play of *Hamlet*, older even than *The Murder of Gonzago*. What Hamlet has done in the closet scene is to cast the experience of the play into the dramatic mode of their common source, to rewrite *Hamlet* into a morality play.

The archaic aspect of *Hamlet*, though it is most conspicuous in the closet scene, is by no means confined to it but pervades the entire play. It enters *Hamlet* with the Ghost, not only the spirit of the elder Hamlet but in a sense the spirit of an older dramatic mode, whose account of recent events in Denmark is told from the eschatological point of view of the medieval drama: the "serpent" Claudius, having wrought King Hamlet's fall in his "orchard," proceeds under the figure of "lust" to "court" the "radiant angel" Gertrude "in a shape of heaven" and work her "falling-off" as well. Hamlet inherits not only his father's name, but his talent for writing morality plays. We could point out that the language in which Hamlet addresses Ophelia in the nunnery scene—"You jig, you amble, and you lisp" (III.i.150)—is not that of psychic derangement but of a preaching Virtue addressing a personification of Vanity or Lechery on the medieval stage. Or we could point to Claudius' account of his fratricide during his futile attempt to pray, a speech explicitly recalling the desperate utterances of Cain after he has murdered Abel in the mystery cycles. But these and other moments in *Hamlet* when the forms and figures of an older drama stand out from the more or less naturalistic surface

Hamlet

of the play are really the tips of an iceberg or, more accurately, the protruding tusks of the mammoth preserved within it.

For it is nothing less than the revenge form itself that is archaic, not only in the sense I have already suggested, that the revenge play had been out of fashion for at least five years and just recently revived when Shakespeare turned to it again around 1600, but in a more fundamental sense as well. This deeper archaism is already implicit in some lines from *The Spanish Tragedy*, spoken by Hieronymo after he has conceived and cast his own revenge play-within-the-play and echoed by Hamlet after the success of *The Murder of Gonzago*:

> Now shall I see the fall of Babylon,
> Wrought by the heavens in this confusion.
> And if the world like not this tragedy,
> Hard is the hap of old Hieronymo.[4]

Hieronymo, like Gertrude, might seem merely to speak figuratively, but his lines too reflect actual stage tradition. In the Protestant morality *Three Laws* (1530-36), for example, the figure of Vindicta Dei drives the chief Vice, Infidelity: off the stage with fire from heaven for what God calls his "Babylonical popery."[5] In the Marian *Respublica* (1553), it is the figure of God's Nemesis who finally brings down judgment on the Protestant Vices, Avarice, Insolence, and Oppression, and restores the commonwealth to "tholde goode eastate."[6] The figure of Divine Correction plays a similar role in Lindsay's *Satire of the Three Estates* (1535-40). In so far as the corrupt courts of the Elizabethan revenge play are pseudohistorical counterparts to the typological Babylon, Sodom, and Gomorrah of medieval drama, its

---

[4] *The Spanish Tragedy*, ed. Philip Edwards (The Revels Plays, Cambridge, Mass., 1959), p. 108.

[5] John Bale, *Three Laws*, ed. J. S. Farmer (Tudor Facsimile Texts, London, 1908), leaf F5r.

[6] *Respublica*, ed. W. W. Greg (E.E.T.S., London, 1952), p. 66.

revenger-heroes are the natural and naturalized offspring of Vindicta Dei and God's Nemesis. Like Hieronymo, most Elizabethan revengers see themselves as scourges of God, legitimate heirs to those Virtue-figures who have divine authorization to commit whatever acts are required to set right the disjointed world, even if the command of a ghost is not quite the same thing as that of God. (A recent analogue is the "licence to kill" conferred on its agents by the modern state in the coldwar reincarnation of the medieval *psychomachia*, the spy novel.) From Hamlet's early assertion that "the time is out of joint; O cursed spite / That ever I was born to set it right" (I.v.189-190) to his parting remarks to his mother that

> Heaven hath pleas'd it so,
> To punish me with this, and this with me,
> That I must be their scourge and minister
> (III.iv.173-175)

he commits himself to a role and a form by their very nature anachronistic. Yet Hamlet's attempt to recast his experience into a morality play is actually half accomplished before he even begins, at least to the extent that the Elizabethan revenge play grows out of native morality tradition, a much greater extent than our preoccupation with Seneca would suggest.[7]

---

[7] See J. W. Cunliffe, *The Influence of Seneca on Elizabethan Tragedy* (Oxford, 1893); F. L. Lucas, *Seneca and Elizabethan Tragedy* (London, 1922); T. S. Eliot, introduction to *Seneca: His Tenne Tragedies*, ed. Thomas Newton (London, 1927). A reaction against the Senecan influence alleged by these proponents begun by Howard Baker, *Introduction to Tragedy* (New York, 1939), has been more fully and persuasively argued by Peter Ure, "On Some Differences between Senecan and Elizabethan Tragedy," *DUJ*, XLI (1948), 17-23, and by G. K. Hunter, "Seneca and the Elizabethans: A Case-Study in 'Influence,'" *ShS* (1966), 17-26. The entire matter has been recently reviewed by Anna Lydia Motto and John R. Clark, "Senecan Tragedy: A Critique of Scholarly Trends" in *Renaissance Drama VI*, ed. Alan C. Dessen (Evanston, 1973), pp. 219-236.

Hamlet

There is, then, an important sense in which the legendary *Ur-Hamlet*, the crude old native play on the subject alluded to by Thomas Nashe and searched for in vain by generations of scholars, is very much alive in the midst of Shakespeare's *Hamlet*. This is not to suggest, however, that Shakespeare borrows nothing from English Seneca. On the contrary, Hamlet tries out classical roles for himself and those around him at several points in the play, but usually in such a way as to reveal their inappropriateness to his situation and rule them out as models for his own action. Gertrude, for example, is only too obviously unlike "Niobe, all tears," the type of the mourning queen to whom he ironically compares her, and Claudius is "no more like my father / Than I to Hercules," the paragon of heroic action. Even though the rugged Pyrrhus hesitates for an instant in the pseudo-Senecan speech, pregnant with present analogies, that Hamlet eagerly solicits from the chief player, whatever identification Hamlet may feel is effectively cancelled when Pyrrhus follows through with his regicide. Nor is this to suggest, however, that the native dramatic roles and forms that Hamlet finally falls back on and that seem to fit more comfortably are a perfect fit either. If they were, why would he continue to castigate himself with his own sense of unworthiness, of having so many offenses at his beck, even after he has cast himself in the self-righteous role of an avenging Virtue? As late as the final act, he is still attempting to close any remaining gap between himself and his chosen role, even as the rhetorical nature of that attempt calls attention to the gap and puts into question the propriety of the role: "Does it not, think thee, stand me now upon . . . is't not perfect conscience / To quit him with this arm? / Andis't not to be damned / To let this canker of our nature come / In further evil?" (v.ii.63-70) Clearly Hamlet knows at some level that he is not and can never become the potent abstraction acting out of lofty and impersonal motives that he makes himself out to be, any more than his experience can wholly conform, or be made to conform, to the older

O'erdoing Termagant

scenario of just and perfect vengeance that he tries to turn it into.

At this point in our discussion we seem to be verging upon an older approach to the classic problem of incoherence and archaism in *Hamlet*, the one exemplified by T. S. Eliot in his well-known essay on the subject. There, Eliot postulates a Shakespeare "unable to impose this motive [of the effect of a mother's guilt upon her son] successfully upon the 'intractable' materials of the old play" and a *Hamlet* "superimposed upon much cruder material which persists even in the final form," a play, in sum, that is "most certainly an artistic failure."[8] Eliot's unhappy judgments are worth considering here, if only because they are based on an intuition of Shakespeare's creative process that is so near to and yet so far from the one presupposed in the present essay. He imagines Shakespeare grappling with his archaic sources in the attempt to naturalize, rationalize, and psychologize—generally speaking, to streamline and neoclassicize them—and at least in the case of *Hamlet*, losing the struggle. Our own intuition of the creative or re-creative act that issued in the play also assumes a struggle with the literary past, but one of a more complex nature. It would seem to be Hamlet who is unable to impose successfully the model of an old play upon the intractable material of his present life, and Shakespeare who dramatizes with unfailing control the tragic conflict between his heroic effort to do so and his ironic consciousness that it cannot be done, with the inevitable by-products of hesitation and delay. Hamlet may well be a projection of Shakespeare's creative self, but there is no doubt as to which is *il miglior fabbro*. After all, if this be failure, what in the world of the arts constitutes success?

For even in those Shakespearean plays for which there are no lost ur-versions, we still encounter a no less pervasive

[8] "Hamlet and His Problems," in *Selected Essays* (New York, 1932), p. 123.

Hamlet

archaism and a scarcely less notorious incoherence by naturalistic or neoclassical standards. Iago, for example, whose motives for doing what he does have proved almost as elusive as Hamlet's for not doing what he is supposed to do, emerges from Bernard Spivack's study of the "hybridization" of allegorical and naturalistic drama in the sixteenth century as your old Vice still, hating and intriguing according to conventions older than those which dominate *Othello* as a whole. And Maynard Mack has reformulated the longstanding problem of staging *King Lear* in terms of the conflicting dramatic worlds the play simultaneously inhabits, the one medieval and visionary and the other modern and illusionistic.[9] If the archaism informing *Hamlet* makes it an artistic failure, so too are *Othello* and *Lear*.

The archeological research into Shakespeare's background in the morality plays pioneered by Spivack has taken us well beyond the genetic speculations culminating in Eliot. Perhaps not surprisingly, however, the poet-critic Eliot seems to approach more closely to Shakespeare's creative process than do these more recent scholars. For their work hardly envisions or requires a creative act at all, based as it is on certain misleading assumptions concerning the "evolution" of dramatic forms which derive, in turn, from the theory of the evolution of biological forms, and trail clouds of imagery whence they came. Spivack in particular talks of "hybrid" plays and characters, of "the complex pregnancy of the Elizabethan drama," of how "the great organism [of Shakespeare's work] unfolds its successive stages of maturity," and, most tellingly, of "survivals of the older subject and the older technique" into Shakespearean drama.[10] The implicit evolutionary analogy is misleading in so far as it infers from the fact of change a large, impersonal, and inexorable force of change, a spirit

---

[9] See respectively Bernard Spivack, *Shakespeare and the Allegory of Evil* (New York, 1958), and Maynard Mack, *King Lear in our Time* (Berkeley, 1965), pp. 45-80.

[10] Spivack, pp. 449-453.

of naturalism which, like the spirit of nature in Wordsworth, rolls through all things and irresistibly transforms the Elizabethan drama. Except, that is, for certain survivals, vestiges, or fossils that linger on, inert but not annihilated. In such accounts of the "evolution" of the drama, as in its Darwinian counterpart, the individual *qua* individual is less important than the species; he is the unwitting medium through whom change manifests itself; his options are to adapt or die, hardly options at all. Little allowance is made in Spivack's or other accounts for what might be termed creative evolution, the capacity of the individual to exercise control over the rate and direction of his own adaptation. For the simple fact is that not all contemporary playwrights are equally archaic or naturalistic. The relation of the individual talent, especially though not exclusively a talent the size of Shakespeare's, to available tradition remains unresolved.

The archaic content of Shakespeare's work is vast but, at least as far as we have seen in the case of *Hamlet*, not haphazard. It remains to be demonstrated that virtually any of his plays will yield, on scrutiny, not a wide scattering of fossilized bones and teeth from an earlier era but the almost perfectly preserved mammoth similar to the one we have begun to disinter. One reason I have chosen *Hamlet* as a point of departure, a play usually discussed in terms of revenge—as distinct from morality—tradition, is incidentally to show that *Othello* and *Lear* are not exceptional in their rich and complex relation to morality tradition. They are not special cases, as they have been generally regarded, but typical cases. Moreover, if archaism in Shakespeare were simply an untransmuted residue left behind by the ever-encroaching tide of naturalism, we should expect to encounter more fossils at the beginning of his twenty-year career than at the end. If anything, the opposite is the case: the final romances are now generally recognized to be *more*, not less, archaic than the early comedies. Similarly, the morality skeleton often observed in *Henry IV* of a darkened prince of the world flanked by the Virtues of honor and

Hamlet

justice and the reverend Vices of riot and debauchery[11] is no less visible, though less often noticed, in *Antony and Cleopatra*. In its large outline and certain local details, Richard III's career recalls the rise and fall of several tyrants and child-murderers of the medieval stage—Pharoah, Herod, Cambyses—but so does Macbeth's. *Richard II* can be seen as one more sad story of the death of kings, a medieval *exemplum* of the educative abasement of the high and mighty not unlike those of *A Mirror For Magistrates*; but so too can *King Lear*. This last example suggests a final criticism of Spivack's approach and the starting-point for a new one. In *Richard II*, there is a great deal in the way of scriptural parallels, medieval pageantry, and emblematic scenes and *tableaux*, but most of it radiates outward, as it were, from Richard's own characterization. He is the immediate author of his play's archaic theatricality, as when he stage-manages the challenge at Coventry, compares himself to Christ and his minions to Judases, calls for a looking-glass during his deposition, and so on. We should distinguish, as neither Eliot nor Spivack does, between that archaism which is Shakespeare's and that archaism which is Richard's or Falstaff's or the elder Hamlet's or Hamlet's own. For Shakespeare often surrounds a character with the trappings of an archaic theatricality as a way of identifying him with an older and passing order of things. The evidence suggests that Shakespeare, far from being an unwitting medium of theatrical change through whose pen archaism and naturalism flow in proportions varying with the date of a given play, is rather the deliberate mediator of theatrical change, concentrating his archaism at certain strategic points, fully aware of the outmodedness of the forms and figures at his disposal.

Given so high a degree of self-awareness, independence, and discrimination in Shakespeare's use of older modes, it is

[11] See, for example, J. Dover Wilson, *The Fortunes of Falstaff* (Cambridge, 1944), pp. 15-35. On the influence of the moralities on the Elizabethan history play, see A. P. Rossiter's preface to his edition, *Woodstock: A Moral History* (London, 1946).

O'erdoing Termagant

conceivably within his power to purge his plays of all archaism and give them over altogether to the new naturalism; yet he chooses not to do so. It takes not a Shakespeare to do that but a Beaumont and Fletcher. Instead, Shakespeare does something more truly sophisticated. He invalidates older modes even as he includes them, supersedes them, in the very act of subsuming them. The result is a troubled awareness, shared by Hamlet himself, of the simultaneous resemblance and discrepancy between the play and its older models that is increasingly forced upon us as the action proceeds. In *The Murder of Gonzago*, the archaic center of *Hamlet*, we watch Shakespeare's play approach and embrace, as it were, its own archaic prototype, only to turn and flee it in an almost choreographic pattern of meeting and parting. Hamlet has selected the old play from the repertory of the tragedians of the city for its mirror-relation to the Danish court and inserted "some dozen or sixteen lines" to sharpen that relation. Yet this "knavish piece of work," as Hamlet terms it, with its dumb-show, idealized characters, and grimacing villain right out of the "croaking raven" school of revenge melodrama, seems less than promising as a mirror or model of the Danish court. Its sheer staginess, its dramaturgic and stylistic archaism, separate it widely from the life of Denmark that frames and mocks it. Then, suddenly, Claudius catches his reflection in its cracked and faded glass, and *The Murder of Gonzago* dissolves into Hamlet, becomes for a while indistinguishable from it.

The play is successful beyond even Hamlet's expectations, as almost everyone assumes the role prescribed for him by this older drama. Hamlet throws himself wholeheartedly into the stock and stagy role of Nemesis, of latter-day Vindicta Dei, and delivers a bloodthirsty soliloquy very much in Lucianus' vein:

> 'Tis now the very witching time of night,
> When churchyards yawn, and hell itself breathes out
> Contagion to this world. Now I could drink hot blood.
> (III.ii.406ff)

Hamlet

Settling deeper into this self-righteous role, he proceeds to horrify Samuel Johnson with another soliloquy in which he "contrives damnation for the man he would punish," the godlike office he later executes on Rosencrantz and Guildenstern. He confronts his mother with her prescribed role of fallen but redeemable sinner, which she reluctantly takes on but promises to play out by mending her ways. Claudius meanwhile fulfills his assigned role of unregenerate Vice, and cursed Cain by admitting his crimes and failing in his effort to pray. Even Ophelia casts herself as a latter-day Patient Griselda, the role taken in the subsequent tragedies by Desdemona and Cordelia, the wronged Virtue who must suffer long and be kind, love and be silent, while she waits for her beloved to wake from his madness. The archaic model roughed out by the Ghost, made flesh in *The Murder of Gonzago*, and refined by Hamlet seems for a while adequate to contain the experience of the play.

Yet all these older roles, and the form that adumbrates them, are already beginning to split at the seams under the pressure of events by the time Hamlet embarks for England. By the time he returns, they have all but burst apart. For one thing, Claudius' impulse to pray, to repent of his sins, distinguishes him from those older embodiments of wickedness who were constitutionally unable to do so. This merely confirms something we had suspected all along, for Claudius is never presented to us as the loathesome degenerate Hamlet makes him out to be. (He never appears on-stage drunk, and is far from a groping satyr in his dealings with Gertrude.) Hamlet, in turn, has failed to see that Claudius cannot pray, and thereby misses his chance for revenge; still worse, he goes on to kill the wrong man. The older figure of Vindicta Dei would not have made either mistake, could not have been deceived by appearances as Hamlet has been, for he lived and moved and had his being in a dramatic mode that truly knew not "seems," a world of moral absolutes, of essential reality, in which God's vengeance could not swerve from its proper object. Moreover, by killing

O'erdoing Termagant

Polonius Hamlet has raised his own Nemesis in Laertes, who embraces the role of fire-breathing revenger with more passion but less theatrical skill and moral discrimination than Hamlet. Meanwhile, Patient Griselda has gone mad; she cannot sustain her part. To adapt a phrase from an Ibsen play well to the other side of naturalism, "people don't do such things" in morality plays, but then, that is because they are not presented as people, whose psyches can crack and who take on roles for which they are ill-suited. In the medieval drama there is no gap between the role and the character; the role *is* the character. In *Hamlet*, in Shakespeare, the role and the identity that assumes it are separable, and characters choose roles they cannot play or play well. Such unforeseen repercussions, casualties, and miscalculations would not have occurred in a morality, and few of them in an early revenge play. There, expectation is still governed by recognized convention, and murder, however bloody or grotesque, goes by design. In the more circumstantial world of *Hamlet*, with its "accidental judgments, casual slaughters . . . , purposes mistook / Fall'n on th'inventors' heads" (v.ii.393-396), the conventions and expectations of that programmatic world exist only to be frustrated.

In the Hamlet who returns from his accident-filled and abortive voyage to England, and who talks quietly with Horatio in the hall, awaiting what the interim will bring, many commentators have seen a changed Hamlet. Perhaps one measure of the change in Hamlet is his repudiation of the role in which he had formerly cast himself:

>   Let us know,
> Our indiscretion sometime serves us well
> When our deep plots do pall; and that should learn us
> There's a divinity that shapes our ends,
> Rough-hew them how we will.
>   (v.ii.7-11)

The older model into which he has tried to cast the experience of the play has broken down completely. That

Hamlet

model was originally designed to comprehend the essential reality above or behind the world of appearances in which we live, which from its point of view is sheer illusion. Hamlet lives and dies knowing only "seems"; only God knows "is." In Hamlet's hands, the older model has proved rough-hewn indeed. His efforts to fit the life of Denmark into it have come increasingly to resemble those of the sorcerer's apprentice, or in his own phrase for bad actors, one of "Nature's journeymen," as this self-styled Virtue is indictable by the end of the play for a series of offences ranging from breach of promise through involuntary manslaughter to premeditated murder. The metaphoric "license to kill" of the old figure of Vindicta Dei has long since expired in a dramatic world in which representation entails a fall into interpretation and subjectivity. The protagonist of *Horestes* (1567), first of Elizabethan revengers, is also the last to hold such a license, and even he has trouble qualifying for it.[12] Revengers, in their human fallibility, are now

---

[12] The conflict between Horestes' human identity as his mother's son and his moral role of avenger is projected into successive debates between him and a personified Nature, who tries to dissuade him from matricide, and the Vice Revenge *alias* Courage, who urges him on. This fundamental conflict also underlies those speeches in which he tries to shed his human frailty and assimilate himself to a divine infallibility through a rhetoric of bloodthirsty bravado soon to characterize all stage revengers:

> Me thinkes I fele all feare to fley, all sorrow griefe & payne.
> Me thinkes I fele courage provokes, my wil forward againe.
> For to revenge my fathers death, and infamey so great,
> Oh how my hart doth boyle in dede, with firey perching heat.
> Courage now welcom by the godes, I find thou art in dede,
> A messenger of heavenly goddes, come let us now procede.
> (247-252)

Although his human fallibility is suggested by his mistaking the Vice for a divine agent, he is spared the ultimate anxieties of Hamlet, since it is the Vice who finally murders Clytemnestra offstage. The significance of Pickering's play as an early attempt to adapt allegorical-morality conventions to classical subject-matter cannot be overestimated. The play is not so much a "missing link" between the drama of

doomed to be hero-villains. The metaphoric license to kill could exist only in a dramatic mode itself a sacred metaphor. Hamlet's attempt to re-enact such a role in a world in which all metaphor is poetic and therefore problematic had been an error of theatrical and moral anachronism. He has tried to be a two-dimensional character in a three-dimensional world.

Throughout the final act Hamlet does his best to salvage the morality play he has vainly tried to shape. From the *danse macabre* of the graveyard scene, where kings and clowns, lawyers and gentlewomen mingle indecorously in Hamlet's imagination, to the summoning by death at the end, he mitigates the severity of his earlier vision and earlier role. Against these latest paradigms, the incongruities of that self-rightous posture, now re-enacted by Laertes, become such stuff as parodies are made on. But even in his closing speeches Hamlet does not so much purge himself of all histrionic and directorial impulses—no Shakespearean character ever changes completely—as exchange one archaic model for another, a heroic for a humble role, Vindicta Dei for Everyman:

> You that look pale and tremble at this chance,
> That are but mutes or audience to this act,
> Had I but time (as this fell sergeant, Death,
> Is strict in his arrest) O, I could tell you—
> But let it be. Horatio, I am dead;
> Thou liv'st; report me and my cause aright
> To the unsatisfied.
>
> (v.ii.345-351)

Horatio, always the good scholar, picks up Hamlet's allusion and carries it to its logical conclusion: "Good night, sweet

---

allegory and the drama of naturalism as a haphazard conflation of two incompatible dramatic modes, the product not of an evolutionary moment but of artistic un-self-consciousness. See *The Interlude of Vice (Horestes)*, ed. Daniel Seltzer (Malone Society Reprints, Oxford, 1961), leaf B1r.

Hamlet

prince, / And flights of angels sing thee to thy rest!" (v.ii. 370-371). But in likening Hamlet's death to the salvation of the morality protagonist, perhaps Horatio presses the analogy too far. For it is his *secular* salvation that concerns Hamlet, the "wounded name" that survives him in history. The other world of the morality drama recedes into a purer kind of dumb-show where "silence" reigns. It is within the historical appearances of "this harsh world" that his story will be weighed and he judged. The play leaves behind its final archaic model by ending on a this-worldly note.

Critics still argue over whether Hamlet is finally a hero or a villain, whether Othello in his last great speech asserts Christian humility or heathen bravado, whether Lear dies illuminated or deceived, and whether Macbeth's death "becomes" him in a fair or foul sense. Such questions are central and crucial to the plays that raise them and reflect what is usually called Shakespeare's characteristic balance and ambiguity. No doubt they represent a refinement beyond the days when critics argued about the afterlives of Shakespeare's heroes, but they proceed, I believe, from the same source within the plays. Though I can offer no definitive answers to these questions, I think we are in a better position now to see why they arise in the first place. They arise, I submit, because the older models embedded in the plays cast life as a drama of salvation and damnation, and the repudiation of those older models guarantees that there will be no clear-cut cases of salvation and damnation. The older models raise the questions; their repudiation insures a multiplicity of responses to them. Shakespeare's plays inhabit the gap between things and the pre-ordained meaning of things, between experience and inherited constructs of experience. Edgar's injunction at the end of *King Lear* to "speak what we feel, not what we ought to say" formulates the difference between our responses to the drama of naturalism and the drama of allegory, and might serve as rubric to the history of Shakespeare criticism. We must speak what we feel because Shakespeare's plays no longer

O'erdoing Termagant

dictate what we ought to say; they offer merely cues, hints, signs. Out of the friction between life and the older models designed to contain life is generated not only the heat of critical controversy but the light of Shakespearean meaning.

Just as the study of his "modernity" begins in the study of his literary past, the study of Shakespearean mimesis, surely the most compelling illusion of reality in world literature, begins paradoxically in the study of convention. Any artist, in order to represent life, must resort to the conventions of art, and in so doing, falsify life in so far as art creates a world rival to life's. Yet for art to be moral, to teach as well as delight, it must also be mimetic; we cannot learn from the actions of creatures with whom we have nothing in common, who are not in some degree like us. Shakespeare resolves this paradox by subsuming within his work a recognizably conventional model of life, repudiating that model, and thereby creating the illusion that he uses no art at all, that he is presenting life directly. Of course what he is really presenting is a more complicated model with its own conventions—one of which is the breakdown of convention—a model that, to adopt Samuel Johnson's phrase, opens an appeal from convention to nature. One reverend Vice of the moralities is a coward, that is, he is Cowardice who masquerades as Courage. Falstaff is like this Vice; yet he is also, as Shakespeare makes equally clear, unlike this Vice in so far as he expresses a range of emotion well beyond that of an allegorical abstraction. Critics can then bring to bear on him their various codes of cowardice and courage in this world in the effort to denote him more truly, some concluding that he is, others that he is not, a coward. The important point, however, is that we half-perceive and half-create Falstaff. The miracle of Shakespearean characterization depends finally, not on his modeling his characters on people he knew, but on his opening up inherited dramatic models to invite, even demand, other models of understanding, including those we use on people we know.

Hamlet

It might be objected that, except by spending a lot of time in libraries, we cannot know, the older conventions of character and action from which Shakespeare creatively departs, and therefore cannot recognize those departures and respond to the new meanings they make possible. This is clearly not the case, however, since those older models are not only stored away in libraries but are carried around, as it were, within the plays themselves, and are there to be perceived by the learned and unlearned alike. The most cursory acquaintance with the tradition of Shakespearean interpretation will turn up ample evidence of the naive identification of the play with its models by the most learned scholars, of the failure to perceive its implicit critique of and departure from those models. And those of us who teach will acknowledge that relatively unlearned students are capable of highly sophisticated distinctions between conventional and unconventional language and conduct within the same play. More often than not, however, these naive and sophisticated responses will co-exist within the same reader, and the process of literary education may well be one of sophisticating our naive responses while keeping in touch with them, of developing a sophisticated simplicity of response that mirrors the sophisticated simplicity of literature. This process will go on whether or not we can name the *de casibus* tragedy or revenge melodrama of the first wave encoded within the play that triggers our naive response in the first place, for it is nothing other than the process of interpretation itself. But the literary-historical knowledge that enables us to do so is an invaluable asset to interpretation, since it provides a means of subjecting to fuller and more rigorous scrutiny responses that might otherwise remain intuitive, impressionistic, and unexamined.

CHAPTER 3

Plays Within Plays: *Othello, King Lear, Antony and Cleopatra*

> Who is it that can tell me who I am?
> Lear's shadow.
> —*King Lear*, 1.iv.236-237

THE DEVICE of the play-within-the-play, though fundamental to our attempt to reconstruct from within Shakespeare's tragedies a model for interpretation at once literary and historical, is of course not an exclusively tragic convention. It occurs, in fact, earlier, more often, and more overtly in his comedies than in his tragedies, so that some distinction clearly must be made between its tragic and comic uses and potential. The archaic center of *A Midsummer Night's Dream*, for example, is Bottom and company's presentation of "A Tedious Brief Scene of Young Pyramus and His Love Thisby, Very Tragical Mirth." The playlet is hilarious not simply because it is ill-produced, but because it is old-fashioned, what Shakespeare's own play might have looked and sounded like had it been written five or ten years earlier, in the heyday of such pseudo-classical potboilers as *Mucedorus* (1590) and *The Rare Triumphs of Love and Fortune* (1582). By making it unmistakably archaic, with its choric self-commentary, crude personification of stage properties, and frequent collapse into what Bottom admiringly terms "'Ercles' vein," Shakespeare clearly differentiates Bottom's play from his own, so much so that Theseus and the lovers see in it nothing of their own erring humanity and ridicule it mercilessly. Yet Shakespeare also makes sure to enforce a certain generic resemblance between his play and Bottom's—it is neither a satire, nor a history play, nor a revenge play, but a pseudo-classical "interlude" of romantic love, what *A Midsummer Night's Dream*, with its lovers' extravagant posturing, overblown rhetoric, and uncontrolled metamorphoses, at several points practically becomes. When the Princess in *Love's Labour's Lost* describes as "great things laboring [which] perish in their birth" the impending pageant of the nine worthies, Berowne points out that her statement could also be taken as "A right description of *our* sport" (v.ii.519-520). Like that pageant, Bottom's play holds up a mirror, although a distorting mirror, to the mortal folly enacted by the principals themselves. The fact that the playlet turns out to be "tragic" and the play comic does not deny their underlying resemblance, since both outcomes are largely the result of chance. Moreover, the lovers' (in *Love's Labour's Lost*, the courtiers') abject failure to recognize themselves in the mirror it holds up serves only to confirm the self-blindness they have exemplified all along. *Pyramus and Thisby* may not seem much like *A Midsummer Night's Dream* at first glance—that is Theseus' rationalist view ("This is the silliest stuff that ever I heard")—but it is finally not so different from it—that is Hippolyta's owlish recognition ("The best in this kind are but shadows...."). In the early comedies, the inclusion of an internal play would seem to create a movement of recognition opposite to that in *Hamlet*, namely, from a perception of initial discrepancy to one of ultimate resemblance.

Of course it is precisely this recognition, that the best in this kind are but shadows, that leads Shakespeare to recreate old plays from his dramatic tradition for inclusion within his own in the first place. For what is gained by this act of inclusion, even in the comedies where the movement is toward convergence between play and prototype, is an illusion of substance, a realism that has little to do with and far transcends any strict adherence to neoclassical rules. This

Plays Within Plays

inherent mimetic advantage of the play-within-the-play will show up even more clearly if we turn to an example from the histories, where Shakespeare seems to feel a special need (to judge from the strenuous efforts of the chorus of *Henry V* to get us to suspend our disbelief) to bring home the immediacy and reality of people and events supposedly "true" yet historically remote, and known mainly through the disembodied form of narrative chronicles. In the tavern scene of *1 Henry IV*, Falstaff attempts to project his imagined rise to power through his impersonations of king and prince. This would-be vice of kings opens the sketch with an imitation of "King Cambyses' vein" followed by a less stilted, but still archaic, euphuism, and Hal responds with a contrasting, almost Jonsonian, colloquialism culminating in the stunning simplicity of "I do; I will." At that prophetic moment the play-within-the-play dissolves into the play, the subsequent action of which realizes and validates Hal's performance and invalidates Falstaff's. For his purposes, Falstaff has chosen in *Cambises* (1558-1569) just the right model for his present scenario, an historical morality in which the ruler remains subject to the Vice. But Hal has chosen for his own model not the negative example of *Cambises*, but those historical moralities, related to Elizabethan lord-of-misrule pageants, in which the Vice is ultimately expelled and order restored, such plays as *Respublica* (1553), Bate's *King John* (1530-1536) and Skelton's *Magnificence* (1513-1516). These are the archaic prototypes, previewed in the tavern scene, to which *Henry IV* finally conforms through Hal's deliberate, self-conscious, and somewhat cold-blooded actions. Not Cambyses a Harry succeeds, but a Magnificence. From the viewpoint of Hal, and no doubt of England, *Henry IV* is clearly a comical history, not only in its texture but in its structure, and re-enacts the moral and social movement from anarchy to order foreshadowed in the play-within-the-play and the historical moralities on which it is based. For Falstaff, however, *Henry IV* moves distinctly toward tragedy, a movement that is also foreshadowed when his own archaic model in the play-within-the-play breaks down even as he attempts to enact it. The archaic role and form in which he has cast himself prove comically inappropriate, to be sure, but also tragically unworkable within a world whose kings no longer talk like King Cambyses nor act with his flamboyant disregard of consequences.

There is an instructive irony of literary history here, however, that points to a basic difference between comic and tragic endomimesis. Even though both Hal and Falstaff are characterized by reference to older roles that each explicitly re-enacts, it is Falstaff who emerges from these plays as a creature of almost detachable reality, while Hal retains something of the pallor and flatness of his allegorical prototypes. This phenomenon is all the more remarkable, since Hal is the given and actual prince of history, and Falstaff's historical status is nonexistent, or shadowy at best. Of course Hal does show more goodly and attract more eyes, does gain a suggestion of the depth and complexity of a living being, as a result of having his own archaic foils to set him off. He is, as Falstaff, puts it "essentially made without seeming so." Like the lovers and would-be worthies of the earlier comedies, who achieve a dimensionality beyond that of their prototypes while still retaining something of their facelessness and interchangeability, Hal also achieves an illusion of substance from his dramatic interplay with shadows, with figures who have unmistakably passed into literature. For those who heckle or invoke those older figures must necessarily seem more "real" and "live" by contrast, even if the latter are not very unlike the former. The effect is analogous to that of the label on a box of Quaker Oats, where the containing figure seems more vivid than the smaller and receding, but otherwise identical, figures on the box he holds merely by virtue of the fact that he contains them and is not himself contained.

The sense of autonomous reality produced by Falstaff on countless audiences from his performance before Elizabeth onward, however, goes beyond this accrual of depth which is inherent in the process of endomimesis, and from which Lysander, Dumaine, and Hal all profit. We can imagine Falstaff independently of the plays in which he appears as we cannot imagine Hal and the others. Nor does his compelling reality have directly to do, as is often suggested, with the mere fact that Falstaff is so physically "there," so substantial and earthy, whereas Hal is presumably thin, or with the fact that Falstaff is morally corrupt whereas Hal is finally virtuous, since vice is allegedly more vivid than virtue. Obviously, there are characters in dramatic literature who equal Falstaff in physical bulk or moral degradation or both, but who are not nearly so vivid and memorable. Falstaff's extraordinary reality arises, I would suggest, out of his tragic situation within the comical history in which he appears, out of his felt discrepancy between the archaic role he so strenuously and imaginatively clings to and a world in which it and he are hopelessly outdated and out of place. He is determined to "play out the play" when it is increasingly clear that it is the wrong play at the wrong time. This sense of impropriety and strain stands in contrast not only to the harmonious relation between his Vice-prototypes and their dramatic worlds but to Hal's harmonious relation to his, since Hal is never under strain and fully capable at any point of "redeeming time when men least think I will." The role and form Hal projects for himself are only too easily realized. He is in the habit of regarding Falstaff as a foil to himself, but in respect of their relative realism Hal functions as a foil to Falstaff. Because comedy moves toward convergence between play and prototype—its traditional happy ending can be seen in literary-historical terms as the joy of marriage or reunion with its own primitive mythic form—it is at once the most conservative of dramatic modes and the one in which the possibility of realism is limited from the start and therefore never really at issue. Hence the readiness with which Shakespeare's comedies and romances are charged with escapism, and the unwillingness of audiences to take

Othello, King Lear, Antony and Cleopatra

comedy in general too "seriously." The "realistic" characters of Shakespeare's comedies—Falstaff, Shylock, and to a lesser degree, Malvolio and Caliban—are invariably tinged with tragedy, beset by a fatal discrepancy between the fictive structures they live by and the fictive world they live in, and are in that sense detachable from and imaginable outside the world of their plays. Conversely, it is in the criticism of the tragedies, the plays in which such discrepancies are central and determining, that characters tend to be discussed as if they were real people and their plays as if they were life. Any theory of Shakespearean representation must take account of this generic difference, with the tragedies offering a more complex use of older forms and more subtle possibilities of mimetic effect than the comedies.

The present study will be confined, in the interest of this greater theoretical challenge, to the tragedies. But given the potential scope of even this foreshortened project, it will have to be confined still further to the group of mature tragedies which A. C. Bradley termed "the famous four": *Hamlet, Othello, King Lear,* and *Macbeth*. This restriction of focus within the tragedies reflects more than the pragmatic need to limit what is still a vast subject. For it is toward these particular tragedies that the kind of mimetic criticism described above, such as Bradley's, which discusses characters as people and plays as life has inevitably gravitated. They have become as a group almost synonymous with "Shakespearean tragedy," which means, in terms of our argument, that the process by which all Shakespearean mimesis works attains in them its most concentrated and complete effect. Virtually no major role remains uncast, no crucial action unmythologized, under older models of conduct drawn primarily from native tradition. The resulting impression is that Shakespeare's principals seem to write their own plays, with little or nothing apparently imposed or contrived by the author. They have the supreme ability to draw other characters, though significantly not everyone, into active, voluntary, and imaginative participation in their designs, thus achieving a coherent recreation of an older drama within the drama itself, even when no play-within-the-play as such is presented. It is almost as if Shakespeare turns the task of writing his tragedies over to his principals, who are not only "poets," as is often remarked, but *dramatic* poets, thereby achieving his own celebrated anonymity or "negative capability" and his equally celebrated impression of effortlessness or naturalness. By the same token, his principals are or become highly self-conscious playwrights, who generally come to perceive the inadequacy of the designs and roles they adopt to direct their destinies and determine their identities. It is this very theatrical self-consciousness that underlies what is traditionally termed "tragic knowledge" or "self-discovery," the capacity to grow or change in the course of enacting their plays we often attribute to Shakespeare's tragic protagonists, that sets them apart from the creatures of lesser dramatists, and that makes their experience more than a purely negative movement toward alienation and death.

To illustrate how this process of self-conventionalization can turn into a process of self-realization, let us turn first to the tragedy most unmistakably modeled on a traditional form. Even though the morality-play within *Othello* is present through allusion rather than presented by inclusion, this fact has not stopped critics from recognizing and responding to it. For those with an archeological interest in Shakespeare, the recognition that Iago resembles the Vice of the moralities is an invaluable aid in discovering coherence in language and conduct that would have to be considered insane by naturalistic or psychological norms. Iago's gleeful self-revelations to the audience, his self-contradictions in setting forth a bewildering array of motives, and his casualness, even lightheartedness, in enacting what is supposed to be a rooted hatred can all be traced back to the behavior of his prototype, the Vice of homiletic and allegorical drama.[1] But to invoke the older convention that governs Iago's behavior, though it may explain *what* he does, cannot satisfactorily explain *why* he does it—unless we are willing to postulate, with Spivack, an involuntary author at the mercy of dramatic evolution or, with Eliot, an incompetent author unable to naturalize his archaic sources. In fact, why Iago acts as he does is not only a problem *of* the play but a problem *in* the play: "Will you, I pray, demand that demi-devil / Why he hath thus ensnared my soul and body?" (v.ii.300-301). As Othello's vocabulary suggests, he has little difficulty recognizing in retrospect the role that Iago has enacted all along; why he has put it on in the first place, however, is the anterior question, which Iago expressly refuses to answer. Moreover, the very fact that Othello finally does recognize the convention which has governed Iago's conduct all along can only mean that for Othello and the rest of the cast Iago's role-playing must have been more than transparently conventional for it to have taken in everyone so completely. This only confirms what virtually any spectator must feel in watching the play, that Iago's behavior, conventional as it may retrospectively seem, manages to transcend mere conventionality and achieve a thoroughly convincing naturalism.

The problem of why Iago casts himself in the role of the Vice in the first place thus leads to the related problem, also unaddressed and insoluble by a purely archeological criticism, of why he succeeds so easily and totally in enacting that role. Why, that is, should Othello fall such easy prey to his snare? The hero of another Elizabethan domestic tragedy contemporaneous with *Othello*, Thomas Heywood's *A Woman Killed with Kindness* (1603), in an almost identical situation demands and gets an "ocular proof" far more compelling—he is shown his wife in bed with his friend—

[1] See Bernard Spivack, *Shakespeare and the Allegory of Evil* (New York, 1958).

Plays Within Plays

before taking action. It does not help in explaining Othello's extraordinary credulity to look for some naturalistic or psychological basis for it in his characterization, such as his supposed jealousy, since no such flaw is visible in him before Iago's overtures. In fact, Iago himself is somewhat surprised at their success: "Can he be angry? . . . And is he angry?" (III.iv.134-137). What is visible in Othello is a marked propensity to allegorize his experience in other-worldly terms, to define his being in terms of the same morality structure that sustains Iago. For Othello is an allegorist, not a literalist, throughout the play and as such is ready at any point to assimilate the natural and human world to a world of abstract and unchanging values. The storm at sea is an apocalyptic storm of winds that "blow till they have wakened death," of seas that rise and "duck again as low / As hell's from heaven," and the reunion with Desdemona, his "soul's joy" and a "content so absolute" (II.i.182-189). Othello lives and moves and has his being within an allegorical mode in which sign and significance are inseparable, words and deeds magically and instantaneously joined. All Iago need do is supply in detachment a few appropriate visual and verbal signs—some muttered misgivings, a few vivid images, a misplaced handkerchief—for Othello to conjure up their referential "reality" for himself, an eternal plot of sin and the wages of sin. The action he undertakes against the "fair devil" Desdemona thus become for him not a "murder" but a "sacrifice," not personal revenge but divine justice: "It is the cause, it is the cause. . . . / O balmy breath, that dost almost persuade / Justice to break her sword" (V.ii.1-17). The morality design that informs *Othello* is the collaborative product of its two principal characters.

The temptation at this point is to accept this allegorization of character and action at face value, to see the play simply as a re-presentation of a timeless or mythic or archetypal—and therefore "true"—pattern in human affairs. Iago becomes of course the incarnation of evil, Othello the tragic human scapegoat, and Desdemona the embodied principle of goodness and patience doomed to suffer long and be kind. The fact that it would not be implausible to place Othello rather than Desdemona in the Christ-like role of persecution and sacrifice should at least alert us to the difficulties involved in such a critical procedure. For to allegorize the play or, more accurately, to return it to its allegorical prototype is to mystify it, to make it illustrate what St. Paul termed the "mystery of iniquity" and leave it at that. Whereas medieval poets may predetermine the meaning of their work by including the exegetical apparatus of allegory within it, this is not what we expect from modern writers, who may well suggest interpretive viewpoints on their work from within it but without curtailing the interpretive freedom of their audience. Nor is it what we expect from Shakespeare, whose work forms a kind of interface between medieval and modern literature. To mystify *Othello* by reducing it to the allegorical drama enacted and expressed by its two main characters, with perhaps some lip-service to its "fleshing out" or naturalization of this basically allegorical structure, is to beg the critical questions with which we began. Why does Iago, or for that matter Othello, adopt an allegorical outlook on his world to begin with, and why, for all their self-conventionalization and self-allegorization, does their play strike us as more than or other than conventional and allegorical?[2]

[2] The possibility of reducing the play to Christian allegory and its characters to moral abstractions is well illustrated, not in the case merely of *Othello* but of all the tragedies, by Roy W. Battenhouse, *Shakespearean Tragedy: Its Art and Its Christian Premises* (Bloomington, 1969). On the other hand, the difficulty of escaping allegorization in the effort to discover a modern and psychological meaning in the play is equally well illustrated by Alvin Kernan: "Desdemona and Iago . . . represent two states of mind, two understandings of life, and Othello's movement from one to the other is the movement on the level of character and psychology from Venice to Cyprus, from The City to anarchy. . . . In some ways I have schematized *Othello* as just such a morality play, offering an allegorical journey between heaven and hell or a stage filled with purely symbolic figures. This is the kind

Plays Within Plays

If the question of Iago's motivation cannot be satisfactorily answered in the older terms of allegory, neither can it be answered in the more modern terms of characterization. For it is circular to try to explain the role-playing of the principals by appeal to that which is itself revealed only through their role-playing and therefore inseparable from it. The question would have to be approached in terms of something that exists prior to and outside of their characters and roles and that is thereby capable of conditioning both. That something might be termed the pre-poetic situation out of which Iago and Othello act, since they create their fictive constructs not in a vacuum but from within a social structure which is already in place before Iago hatches a single plot, and about which we learn a great deal before we even lay eyes on Othello. We quickly learn that both characters exist in a marginal relation to the play's dominant Venetian society, and it is this marginality that helps to explain their role-playing. Almost the first information we receive about Othello is that he is an outsider, set apart by background, idiom, and—pre-eminently—color from the Venetian society he serves. Yet he is also clearly at pains to integrate himself within it by outdoing the Venetians themselves, as we see in his scene before the assembled senate, in civility and self-control. As the living symbol of high Venetian culture, Desdemona is not simply a wife to Othello but the legitimating agent of his acculturation. Her loss would thrust Othello outside the structure within which he is now defined and legitimated, however precariously, in his social roles of general, Christian, and husband and back into the dangerous anarchy and isolation of his pre-Venetian and pre-Christian life. Othello recognizes the precariousness of his position and the grace Desdemona reflects on

---

of abstraction of art toward which criticism inevitably moves, and in this case the allegorical framework is very solidly there." Introduction to *Othello*, ed. Alvin B. Kernan (The Signet Shakespeare, New York, 1963), pp. xxxi, xxxiv. The play's allegorical structure, that is, seems to proclaim itself, as Kernan is uneasily aware, only to deny its validity.

him, and expresses this recognition in the form of a drama of salvation and damnation: "Perdition catch my soul / But I do love thee! and when I love thee not / Chaos is come again" (III.iii.90-92). His wholehearted adoption of the dramatic vocabulary of Christian allegory projects his essential relation to the Venetian society that she represents and that he would have adopt him. At the same time, the rhetorical and histrionic overcompensation with which he employs that formal convention and throws himself into its roles reveals the very marginality he would overcome through them.

Though Iago is of course a Venetian, he too exists in a marginal relation to the dominant Venetian society. He serves under "an erring barbarian" and has been passed over in favor of a mere Florentine "arithmetician," another outsider to whom he deems himself superior in all relevant professional categories as well as in intelligence and self-discipline. This is not to suggest, reductively, that Iago does what he does because Othello has made Cassio lieutenant instead of him. That rebuff is merely a symptom of the prior and more fundamental decadence of a social structure that keeps down "merit" and prefers outsiders graced with "letter and affection." Deprived of a social role commensurate with his conviction of superiority, Iago creates a rival structure in which he is central and potent rather than marginal and impotent, one through which he can demonstrate the very subordination of passion to reason he prides himself on and finds wanting in everyone around and above him:

> The power and corrigible authority . . . lies in our wills. If the balance of our lives had not one scale of reason to poise another of sensuality, the blood and baseness of our natures would conduct us to most prepost'rous conclusions. But we have reason to cool our raging motions, our carnal stings or unbitted lusts, whereof I take this that you call love to be a sect or scion.
>
> (I.iii.320-328)

Plays Within Plays

Iago's "psychology" takes the form of an anatomy of the soul whose terms are taken over from countless morality plays, and which no medieval or renaissance theologian would dispute. Except, that is, for its glaring omission of grace and reduction of love, all exogenous and redemptive functions having been displaced entirely onto the self and replaced by the "authority" of the individual will. The morality play he creates is thus a slick perversion of the values of his own Venetian and Christian culture and of the traditional form that embodies those values. From his own point of view, however, the bewildering multiplicity of Iago's motives becomes intelligible in their very multiplicity. To assert "authority" is to "plume up my will" (I.iii.384), a process that requires an object, or better still, as many objects as possible, since one cannot simply will but must will *something*. Given the primacy of the will, its particular objects must always be arbitrary, *ad hoc*, and of secondary concern. But what better objects than the passionate creatures around him, whom he proceeds to caricature into veritable monsters of appetite leaping almost at random into each other's beds, and who are living symbols of the social structure that keeps him subservient?

The point is that the play presents not only its own allegorization but the basis for demystifying that allegory, the situational logic out of which Iago's and Othello's impulse to allegorize themselves in the first place can be seen to arise. The question remains, however, of why Iago and Othello are discussed as if they were the autonomous and impenetrable figures out of the world of allegory they make themselves out to be, when the play provides the basis for rendering them accessible and interpretable in this-worldly terms. This acceptance of the principals' self-allegorization is not really surprising when we consider how unanalytical and acquiescent the rest of the cast is. The web that Iago and Othello spin around themselves is only reinforced by the others, who are at once too closely enmeshed in it and too prone to allegorizing themselves to see it as allegory.

Othello, King Lear, Antony and Cleopatra

So absorbed are Desdemona and Cassio in projecting and enacting roles for themselves—the role of patient virtue who refuses to commit adultery "for the whole world," who takes the guilt of her world on herself ("A guiltless death I die"), and who forgives even her own murderer; and the role of innocent idealist with his own Othello-like "daily beauty in his life" and his own Petrarchan adoration of "the divine Desdemona"—that neither is in a position of sufficient detachment to question or probe either his own motives or those of others:

> *Othello.* How comes it, Michael, you are thus forgot?
> *Cassio.* I pray you pardon me. I cannot speak.
> (II.iii.178-179)

> *Emilia.* He called her whore....
> *Iago.* Why did he so?
> *Desdemona.* I do not know; I am sure I am none such.
> (IV.ii.119-123)

The characters of the play provide the cue for their own mystification in their inability to step back from or outside of the roles they equate with themselves. In this respect, Roderigo is comically paradigmatic of the rest in his relation to "honest Iago." He is so caught up in his own role of languishing lover that he cannot see the blatant contradiction between Iago's stated disdain of "passion" and his professed commitment to furthering Roderigo's passion.

There is one character, though, who is constitutionally unassimilable into the delicate web constructed by Iago and ultimately responsible for its unraveling. That foreign body is Emilia, in her worldliness and pragmatism a walking contradiction of the others' allegorizing sensibilities, a fugitive from the alien and anti-allegorical tradition of Italian comedy, and a natural demystifier of all allegorical projects. Samuel Johnson's famous remark that Emilia "wears her virtue loosely, but does not cast it off" suggests something of her anti-allegorical nature, her unique status within a dra-

Plays Within Plays

matic world where everyone else is tightly wrapped up in moral role-playing. In the end, it is Emilia who refuses to "charm her tongue" in deference to Othello's dignifying his act as a "sacrifice," or to shield her own husband, as Desdemona does hers, in an act of self-effacing loyalty. Instead, she demystifies their role-playing by exposing the gross errors and mistaken identities, the incongruous comic underside, of the transcendent action they have staged. Othello's role of "justice" and act of "sacrifice" are reduced by Emilia to a sordid murder by a jealous "fool," a "gull," a "dolt / As ignorant as dirt." Iago's demonic pretentions are also deflated by Emilia's squabbling account of his lies and thievery: " 'Tis proper I obey him, but not now." For her the handkerchief is neither a magical symbol nor a theatrical prop, but a mere object, a "trifle" significant only for the disproportionate interest Iago had expressed in having it. The *denouement* of the play, the unraveling of the web that results from Emilia's breathless revelations, brings us very close to a complete demystification of the word-magic on which Iago's design has depended: "Let heaven and men and devils, let them all, / All, all, cry shame against me, yet I'll speak." Even Othello himself seems, at least for a moment, to repudiate the superstitious or sacramental mentality that has brought him to this point: "I look down towards his feet—but that's a fable."

Yet this movement of the play toward what can only be called de-allegorization is simultaneously a movement toward re-allegorization. The very language in which Emilia deflates Othello's self-dramatization, though it has a certain parodic excess and responds to his own language, is still very much within the prevailing convention: "O, the more angel she, / And you the blacker devil!"; "Thou dost belie her, and thou art a devil"; "O, she was heavenly true" (v.ii.129-130, 132, 134). This is Gratiano's idiom too, when he remarks that had Brabantio been alive to look on, he would "curse his better angel from his side / And fall to reprobation" (v.ii.205-206). It is true that these re-allegorizations come before a full disclosure of events has occurred, but, even afterward, Iago can remystify himself in a phrase when he answers Othello's taunt and sword-thrust—"If that thou be'st a devil, I cannot kill thee"—with the still magic words, "I bleed, sir, but not killed" (v.ii.202-203). Neither the devil, it would seem, nor the mode of vision the perceives him clothed in human flesh, dies so easily after all. Othello has already gone through several roles from the morality repertory: an Everyman precariously poised between "content" and "perdition" on his arrival in Cyprus; a figure of unwavering justice once his doubt is replaced by resolution; and now, in the logic of his own allegorization, a damned sinner: "Whip me, ye devils, / From the possession of this heavenly sight! / Blow me about in winds! roast me in sulfur!" (v.ii.274-276). The scene is identified, through Othello's invocations of "a huge eclipse" and "stones in heaven," with the Last Judgment itself.

The process of de-allegorization and re-allegorization is not yet over, however, and the process of realization that paradoxically arises from it has yet to emerge fully. For what is Othello's great and controversial final speech but a renewed effort to define himself and Desdemona by assimilating them both to a new set of roles?

> Soft you, a word or two before you go.
> I have done the state some service, and they know't.
> No more of that. I pray you, in your letters,
> When you shall these unlucky deeds relate,
> Speak of me as I am. Nothing extenuate,
> Nor set down aught in malice. Then must you speak
> Of one that loved not wisely, but too well;
> Of one not easily jealous, but, being wrought,
> Perplexed in the extreme; of one whose hand,
> Like the base Judean, threw a pearl away
> Richer than all his tribe; of one whose subdued eyes,

Plays Within Plays

> Albeit unused to the melting mood,
> Drop tears as fast as the Arabian trees
> Their med'cinable gum. Set you down this.
> And say besides that in Aleppo once,
> Where a malignant and a turbaned Turk
> Beat a Venetian and traduced the state,
> I took by th' throat the circumcised dog
> And smote him—thus.
>
> (v.ii.334-352)

The speech begins by recapitulating, in answerable style, the roles we have already seen him run through: plain-speaking soldier ("No more of that"); conventional lover of sonnet tradition ("one that loved not wisely, but too well"); divinely moved revenger ("perplexed in the extreme"); and the transcendent murderer he has now become ("of one whose hand. . . ."). It is this final role that defies, in his effort to present himself "as I am" and avoid extenuation, a perfunctory summing-up. Once again, Othello does not so much present himself as re-present himself; that is, he defines and identifies himself through a dazzling series of emblematic figures.

There is a crucial difference, however, between this last effort at self-allegorization and his previous efforts, in that these latest roles no longer have the rigidity and clarity of outline of his earlier roles, but melt into and blur one another, like superimposed images vying to occupy the same space. Is Othello now to be identified with the infidel Turk or with the defender of the faith and the state who punished him? With the avenger or the victim? With Judas or Christ? Even the notorious textual crux (the folio "Indian" or the quarto "Judean"?) fortuitously adds to the effect of ultimate ambivalence, since we cannot know whether Othello designates himself a benighted Indian (that would recover for him a radical innocence) or a treacherous Judean like Judas or Herod (that would convict him of apocalyptic ignorance). His very last lines—"I kissed thee ere I killed

Othello, King Lear, Antony and Cleopatra

thee, no way but this, / Killing myself to die upon a kiss"—would seem to reinforce the reading of himself as Judas, but they could also be read as an extension of his earlier Petrarchanism, a conventional figure now made grimly literal. His final speech and gesture can only point inward toward an indefinite antecedent, a radical self that remains humanly impossible to denote truly. He has reinvented his own earlier dramatic language with a new understanding that prior sign and present significance, conventional role and distinctive self, can never fully coincide, and creates in the process a more authentic, because more human, magic than that displayed in any of his previous rhetoric of self-definition. Of course this final speech is also a remystification of himself, since it remains within the realm of role-playing. Yet it is also a demystification of the self, since it calls attention through the sheer diversity and internal tension of the roles it invokes to its own process of self-definition. Othello can even be seen at this point as something of a tragic Bottom, wishing to play all the roles himself—avenger, scapegoat, witness—and making a mockery of them all. Critics as early as Rymer and as recent as Eliot have in fact advanced this view. Yet the authenticity they would deny can be reasserted, in the cases of both *Bottom* and *Othello*, by shifting its basis from the product to the process, by appeal, that is, to an impulse to self-dramatization that is itself definitive of the human condition, however inexact or inappropriate the results of this dreaming or playing turn out to be. After all, the best in this kind are but shadows. Clearly the interpretive possibilities for demystifying and remystifying Othello and *Othello* are bottomless, yet it is precisely their ultimate indeterminacy in relation to their earlier models that sets them apart from those models and makes them unconventional and lifelike. We are left with a character and an action "true" in their acknowledged indeterminacy and indeterminate in their presented truth.

The fluctuaton between demystification and remystification we have traced in *Othello* is not a function of the unbridled ingenuity of the interpreter. For this fluctuation is neither lawless nor idiosyncratic. It is controlled by the poles of allegory and parody built into the very structure of the tragedies as imitations or re-presentations of earlier actions, to which the interpreter more or less self-consciously responds. This is why criticism of the tragedies tends to arrange itself around a central issue or problem within a given play—the problem of delay in *Hamlet* or of motivation in *Othello*—and why no conclusive solutions to these problems ever seem to appear and thereby end the debate. The classic interpretive problems of the tragedies, that is, locate precisely those places where an older mode of comprehending human conduct appears at odds with the conduct Shakespeare presents. Thus, a critic aware of Shakespeare's dramatic tradition, such as Spivack or even Eliot, will seek to resolve the problematics of the tragedies in terms of their tradition, often by reducing the play to a repetition of its prototype and ignoring or overlooking its crucial divergence from it. Conversely, a critic without specific knowledge of Shakespeare's dramatic tradition such as Coleridge, will tend in his reflections to identify the play with its cruxes, as if it were *all* divergence and modernity, an autonomous and unmediated action without artistic precedent. The former might be termed the conservative, or pious, or, as I have already called it, archeological approach, and the latter the romatic, or modernist, or even characterological approach, since it tends, for reasons gone into at the outset of this discussion, to concentrate on the prince at the expense of the poem. The pious or conservative approach, which in fact dominates a chronologically later period in the history of Shakespearean criticism, demystifies the tragedies by attempting to explain them in terms of their tradition. But it also remystifies them by presupposing a fundamentally unself-conscious author through whom the impersonal voice of tradition speaks for itself. The romantic approach, while demystifying the tragedies

Othello, King Lear, Antony and Cleopatra

by treating their principals as real people not unlike you and me (Coleridge: "I have a smack of Hamlet myself"), also remystifies them by endowing their creator with an autonomous, even divine, power of origination (Hugo: "Next to God, Shakespeare created most"). Yet both possibilities of response, as we have seen in *Othello*, are implicit in the tragedies themselves, are actually inscribed into them, and arise as a consequence of their radically ambivalent status as *structures which can never quite reunite with their own dramatic models nor leave those models definitively behind.*

The ways in which a play's central interpretive problem arises from specific changes Shakespeare has wrought on his traditional models are particularly clear and traceable in the case of *King Lear*. At least as early as Samuel Johnson's pained observations on the ending of the play, interpretation has concerned itself with what to make of Shakespeare's alteration of the traditional story of Lear and Cordelia away from poetic justice and toward unprecedented suffering. As everyone knows, all of Shakespeare's immediate sources—the old play *King Leir*, Holinshed's *Chronicles*, Spenser's *Faerie Queene*, and *A Mirror for Magistrates*—present Lear and Cordelia triumphant at last, with virtue rewarded and vice punished. Though some versions return Cordelia to prison, the victim of further rebellion and finally her own suicide, these events occur after Lear's vindication and peaceful death. Moreover, Shakespeare has made other changes which would seem to redouble the deliberate violence of this basic change. For one thing, he has omitted the wealth of consoling Christian and Biblical parallels that interlace the play of *Leir*, as well as most of the Christian atmosphere that permeates the other versions. Then too, he has included the parallel subplot of Gloucester and his sons, derived from Sidney's *Arcadia*, and apparently serving to universalize and underscore the cruelties of the Lear action. As if this were not enough, he adds the ordeal of madness to Lear's other afflictions. It is not difficult to see how these changes encourage the two basic possibilities of response I have termed pious and romantic, each of which informs a school of criticism on the play. A neo-romantic or modernist response oriented toward the result of Shakespeare's alterations of his Christian sources rather than the sources themselves has stressed the godless secularity of the play, the paganness of its world, and the unredeemed or "absurd" nature of its suffering. To a more allegorizing and archeological school, however, it remains possible to see through or past Shakespeare's alterations of his Christian sources in order to reconcile the play with them. "Only to earthbound intelligence," writes one critic, "is Lear pathetically deceived in thinking Cordelia alive. Those familiar with the Morality plays will realize that Lear has found in her unselfish love the one companion who is willing to go with him through Death up to the throne of the Everlasting Judge."[3]

These are of course the extreme possibilities of response to the play. But there is a third possibility, more problematic and interesting in that it combines elements of both the modernist and pious approaches to the play in uneasy suspension. This is the view most fully articulated by A. C. Bradley, who represents the culmination of the romantic approach and sees the implications of Shakespeare's changes in their full horror, yet who also cannot resist suggesting that the play might be piously retitled "The Redemption of King Lear." In his ambivalence Bradley anticipates what has perhaps become the dominant approach to the play, an approach that is not explicitly Christian but that displaces the older Christian meanings into the terms of a secular humanism, the Christian origin and structure of which are still clear. Lear changes, grows, gains wisdom, even a

[3] O. J. Campbell, "The Salvation of Lear," *ELH*, xv (1948), p. 107. A useful review of Christian and existentialist, optimist and pessimist readings of the play is provided by William R. Elton in the opening chapter of his study of its renaissance theological content and context, King Lear *and the Gods* (San Marino, 1966).

kind of redemption as the result of his suffering, madness, and death. Though Cordelia may not be the incarnate principle of Faith or Love, she is the human mediator of those virtues. Through strenuous exegesis along these lines, a critic such as Maynard Mack can argue for the modernity of the play and at the same time re-assimilate it to the vision of redemption offered in its sources, Shakespeare's departures from them serving only to humanize and deepen that vision by making it harder-earned and by that token more valuable:

> If there is any "remorseless process" in *King Lear*, it is one that begs us to seek the meaning of our human fate not in what becomes of us, but in what we become. Death, as we saw, is miscellaneous and commonplace; it is life whose quality may be made noble and distinctive. Suffering we all recoil from; but we know it is a greater thing to suffer than to lack the feelings and virtues that make it possible to suffer. Cordelia, we may choose to say, accomplished nothing, yet we know it is better to have been Cordelia than to have been her sisters. When we come crying hither, we bring with us the badge of all our misery; but it is also the badge of the vulnerabilities that give us access to whatever grandeur we achieve.[4]

Quite apart from the statement itself, Mack's conclusion recalls in its rhetoric of contrast and compensation—"Death . . . life"; "Suffering . . . a greater thing"; "nothing . . . better"; "misery . . . vulnerabilities"—nothing in the play so much as Edgar's own summing-up: "Speak what we feel, not what we ought to say. / The oldest hath borne most: we that are young. . . ." Of course it also recalls the homiletic rhetorical mode of Shakespeare's own Christian sources, not only the old *Leir* and *A Mirror for Magistrates* but the medieval dramatic and visionary tradition that Mack himself discovers behind the play. In the effort to argue the

[4] *King Lear in Our Time* (Berkeley, 1965), p. 117.

play's modernity, its special relevance for "our time," Mack draws our attention, stylistically and substantively, to its most conventional and Christian elements.

What is it, then, in the structure of *King Lear* that moves such critics as Bradley and Mack to reach conclusions manifestly at odds with their own critical premises, the one employing a romantic approach in the service of Christianizing the play, and the other an archeological approach in the name of its presumed modernism? Such paradoxes of critical response can be traced directly to one of the major changes Shakespeare has worked on his sources, the introduction of the story of Gloucester as a reflection of the story of Lear. Bradley was, in fact, among the first to explore the implications of this parallelism, and most commentators since have followed him in seeing its effect as one of mutual reinforcement. The Gloucester subplot, that is, works "to enact and express a further aspect of the Lear experience."[5] It now becomes clearer how the Christianity Shakespeare has apparently taken pains to remove from *King Lear* finds its way back into its interpretation. For

[5] L. C. Knights, "The Question of Character in Shakespeare," in *More Talking of Shakespeare*, ed. John Garrett (London, 1959), p. 66. Quoted with approval by Maynard Mack, p. 71. The *locus classicus* of this view within Shakespearean criticism is to be found in A. C. Bradley: "The secondary plot fills out a story which would by itself have been somewhat thin. . . . This repetition does not simply double the pain with which the tragedy is witnessed: it startles and terrifies by suggesting that the folly of Lear and the ingratitude of his daughters are no accidents or merely individual aberrations, but in that dark cold world some fateful malignant influence is abroad, turning the hearts of the fathers against their children and of the children against their fathers, smiting the earth with a curse, so that the brother gives the brother to death and the father the son, blinding the eyes, maddening the brain, freezing the springs of pity, numbing all powers except the nerves of anguish and the dull lust of life." *Shakespearean Tragedy* (New York, 1904, reprinted 1955), pp. 210-211. Like Mack and most others, Bradley transfers the superstitious or pious view of moral causality expressed by Gloucester onto the Lear action and proceeds to expound that view in the rhetoric of Christian homiletic.

the Gloucester action embodies an essentially Christian structure, or at least a concerted attempt on the part of its principal actors to discover or recreate such a structure:

> *Albany.* If that the heavens do not their visible spirits
> Send quickly down to tame these vile offences,
> It will come,
> Humanity must perforce prey on itself,
> Like monsters of the deep.
> (IV.ii.45-49)

> *Albany.* This shows you are above,
> You justicers, that these our nether crimes
> So speedily can venge. But, O poor Gloucester!
> Lost he his other eye?
> (IV.ii.78-81)

> *Edgar.* It was some fiend; therefore, thou happy father,
> Think that the clearest gods, who make them honors
> Of men's impossibilities, have preserved thee.
> (IV.vi.72-74)

> *Edgar.* The gods are just, and of our pleasant vices
> Make instruments to plague us:
> The dark and vicious place where thee he got
> Cost him his eyes.
> (V.iii.171-174)

Each of these expressions of belief in divine justice and providential purpose—the most explicit in the play—occurs at a major turning point in the plot, but in each instance it is the Gloucester plot that is involved. If the Gloucester plot is supposed to exist in a mirroring or parallel relation to the Lear plot, it becomes not only possible but inevitable that the Christian structure and sentiment expressed through the former will be transferred to the latter, whatever critical premise we start from.

Yet it is precisely the pervasive Christianizing of the subplot that puts into question its supposed parallelism with the main plot. It is almost as if the older Christian structure deliberately dismantled in the story of Lear is just as deliberately reconstructed in the story of Gloucester, which had been only implicitly Christian in Sidney. With its black-and-white contrasts of good and bad, lawful and illegitimate, "natural" and "unnatural" sons, its clear symmetries of cause and effect, sin and retribution, moral blindness and physical blinding, the Gloucester action is basically as simple and homiletic in structure as any of the neat little "tragedies" of *A Mirror for Magistrates* and the long medieval tradition of the falls of illustrious men that lies behind it. The Gloucester action, like the medieval and morality-derived models of the *Lear* action, is not "tragic" at all in the sense we have been exploring. It offers none of the fatal discrepancies between form and experience, role and self, sign and significance that we have seen beset Hamlet and Othello, no heroic casting about for roles and forms to define present experience, and no ironic awareness of their inadequacy even as they are played out. In this respect, the Gloucester-Edgar-Edmund subplot in *Lear* resembles nothing in the earlier tragedies so much as the Polonius-Laertes-Ophelia subplot in *Hamlet*, with which it shares the common function of re-enacting a recognizably conventional "tragedy" that throws the more intractable experience of Hamlet and Lear into stark relief. Just as the Polonius subplot turns out to be a simple revenge melodrama with the stock revenger Laertes as protagonist, as latter-day Nemesis, so the Gloucester subplot turns out to be a simple dramatic *exemplum* illustrating the educative abasement of the complacent sinner. Its essential Christian structure is foreshadowed as early as Kent's casual reply to Gloucester's tasteless jokes over Edmund's bastardizing: "I cannot wish the fault undone, the issue of it being so proper" (1.i.17-18). The action, that is, illustrates a fortunate fall and issues in redemptive suffering, a sadder but wiser man, and a happy death: "his flawed heart . . . 'Twixt two extremes of passion, joy and grief, / Burst smilingly" (v.iii.198-201). The Gloucester action at no point puts into question its initial assumptions concerning the origin of evil or the meaning of suffering, for in its fulfillment of a conventional Christian design those questions are answered in advance and those answers only confirmed by its outcome. Something always comes of something, evil of illegitimacy and good of legitimacy. The universe of the Gloucester action operates by strict and transparent laws of cause and effect, which are at no point challenged, though of course they can be disobeyed: "I stumbled when I saw." The assumption here is that he now sees "feelingly" and truly. Just as his "pilgrimage" to Dover has an attainable goal, though it is not the one he intended, so experience has an ascertainable meaning, though it may not be ascertained until the end.

The Gloucester action is designed throughout to illustrate that meaning, negatively and positively, through the theatrical endeavors of Edmund and Edgar. For their histrionics, though morally contrasting, are always of a distinctly programmatic and emblematic kind. Their role-playing, that is, is only skin-deep. In Edgar's appearance as Poor Tom and later as unnamed challenger, there is nothing of the groping toward self-definition we associate with Shakespearean tragic role-playing. His roles are as easily and completely put on and off as the costume or vizor they depend on: "Edgar I nothing am" (II.ii.21). They are mere expedients contrived for the temporary purpose of preserving himself, bringing Gloucester through despair to repentance, and recovering his own legitimate rights, and once they have successfully achieved those purposes they are shed as the mere disguises they are. Edmund's role-playing is equally superficial. There is none of the mystery behind his Vice-like plot of ambition and intrigue that there is in the case of Iago, with whom he is often misleadingly equated. Edmund's "motivation" is only too clear from the patronizing treatment we see him receive at Gloucester's hands and from his own soliloquy on his status as bastard.

Plays Within Plays

To be a bastard is, as Edmund makes clear, to be superfluous, to have no rightful or legal place within the social structure. He *therefore* attempts to legitimate himself in the name of an amoral nature that exists prior to social forms, to create a rival structure proceeding from and centered on the self. All this is perfectly logical, as Richard III's "And *therefore*, since I cannot prove a lover. . . / I am determined to prove a villain" (*Richard III*, I.i.28-30) is logical. But in neither case is it psychological; it points to no hidden depths. Edmund has in fact more in common with such early and morality-derived Shakespearean villains as Aaron the Moor, Don John, and Richard III, who carry around with them an external sign or stigma that serves as badge and pretext for their villainy, than he does with Iago, whose alienation goes deeper and carries no badge, who is at some level a mystery to himself, and whose cultivation of a Vice-like evil can be neither fully explained nor fully demystified. For unlike that of Iago, Edmund's role can be put off as easily as it was put on: "Yet Edmund was beloved . . . some good I mean to do / Despite of mine own nature" (v.iii.241-246). Of course the scene of Edmund's "reformation" is no less naturalistic, no more openly homiletic in conception and derivation, than the scene of Gloucester's "suicide" and "salvation" stage-managed by Edgar. But then, these moments are not to be regarded as lapses on the part of a Shakespeare aiming at naturalistic consistency but here and there falling short of his mark. For it is within the Gloucester action that these "lapses," which are part and parcel of its homiletic structure, moral emblematization, and allegorical motivation, are largely confined.[6] The air of contrivance that hangs about the Gloucester action is pervasive, and it smells of morality.

[6] Bradley, for example, lists a number of "improbabilities" and "inconsistencies" in the play: Edmund's ruse of writing a letter when he and Edgar live in the same house; Gloucester's journey to Dover to destroy himself when he might have done it closer to home; Edgar's unexplained decision not to reveal himself to his father; and so on.

Othello, King Lear, Antony and Cleopatra

Why, then, is the Gloucester action not more generally recognized to be deliberately archaic and artificial but is discussed instead as if it possessed or ought to possess a naturalistic coherence comparable to that of the Lear action? Here again the presupposition of a mutually reinforcing parallelism between the two plots is the source of potential misinterpretation. Just as the assumption of parallelism tempts us to expect from the Lear action a Christian allegorical coherence it does not have, so too it tempts us to expect from the Gloucester action a naturalistic coherence and dimensionality it does not have. Edgar's rhyming conclusion to the play, for example, in which he enjoins all present to "speak what we feel, not what we ought to say," is often cited and discussed as if it constituted a deep and authentic response to the play's tragic experience and confirmed Edgar's wisdom and humanity. This is particularly ironic and revealing in so far as the speech may well belong to Albany—only the folio assigns it to Edgar—and it would make little difference if it were spoken by Albany. For quite apart from its choric conventionality familiar from previous summings-up by the likes of Horatio and Fortinbras, Cassio and Lodovico, the speech actually indicts its own speaker and its own idiom for having consistently done just the opposite. Edgar and Albany, who serve within the play as interpreters of Gloucester's experience, have throughout traded in a consoling and instructive morality with an unself-questioning assurance and an easy credulity that puts into question what it is they feel and whether they feel at all. Albany's assertions, for example, of divine justice—"This shows you are above / You justicers . . . But, O poor Gloucester! / Lost he his other eye?"—or his re-assertion at the end of its secular counterpart—"All friends shall taste / The wages of their virtue, and all foes / The

---

Bradley does state, however, that the improbabilities he lists are "particularly noticeable in the secondary plot." *Shakespearean Tragedy*, pp. 207-208.

Plays Within Plays

cup of their deservings. O, see, see!" (v.ii.304-306)—are dramatically undermined by events that would seem blatantly to contradict them: the loss of Gloucester's other eye, the death-pangs of Lear. But when faced with the choice between revising their Christian vision in the face of adverse experience and simply reasserting that vision, such characters as Albany and Edgar invariably choose the latter course, persist in speaking what they "ought to say" at the expense of what they "feel." Or perhaps for such determined moralists there is finally no consciousness of a gap between saying and feeling, since their action is shaped by them precisely to do away with all such discrepancies by containing, in the manner of medieval allegory, its own interpretation within it. The temptation to which many, if not most, commentators on the subplot have succumbed has been to follow their example and suppress their own sense of difference between the voice of convention and the voice of feeling—that is to say, between the subplot and the main plot.[7]

This is not finally to suggest, as up to now I may have seemed to be doing, that Shakespeare has indeed purged the Lear action of all remnants of older Christian dramatic convention. On the contrary, the main action often turns

---

[7] Despite the pervasiveness of the critical tendency to assimilate the two actions to one another, a nagging sense of tonal and structural difference is expressed by some critics. Bradley himself qualifies his assertion of a mutually reinforcing parallelism by stating that the subplot "provides a most effective contrast between its personages and those of the main plot, the tragic strength and stature of the latter being heightened by comparison with the slighter build of the former." *Shakespearean Tragedy*, pp. 210-211. See, for example, Alvin B. Kernan, "Formalism and Realism in Elizabethan Drama: The Miracles in *King Lear*," *Renaissance Drama* IX (1966), pp. 59-66; Sigurd Burckhardt, *Shakespearean Meanings* (Princeton, 1968), pp. 237-259; and Richard Levin, *The Multiple Plot in English Renaissance Drama* (Chicago, 1971), pp. 12-13. The "grotesque awkwardness," "mediacy," and "externality" which these critics respectively find in the subplot are all a function of its deliberate archaism and conventionality in contrast to the main plot.

Othello, King Lear, Antony and Cleopatra

toward conventions of emblem and allegory not essentially different from those that govern the subplot, despite the fact that Shakespeare has in the end denied the poetic justice of his Christian sources. The very first scene of the division of the kingdom, for example, with its emblematic map and ritualistic speeches has struck many as archaic and antinaturalistic, a scene out of fairy-tale. In fact it recalls, in its stylized presentation of kingly pride and folly, the opening scene of one of the oldest extant moralities, *The Pride of Life* (1425) or, closer to home, the opening scene of *Gorboduc* (1562). Like his prototypes, Lear persists, against the admonitions of his wise counselors, in a course that proves disastrous, and, like them too, lives to repent of his actions. Given this initial and basic resemblance between the structure of the play and such models as these, a resemblance that has clearly survived Shakespeare's reworking of his immediate sources, it is little wonder that Bradley and others have glimpsed a vision of redemption in the play. Nor are these resemblances confined to the opening scene or the overarching structure of the Lear action. They reappear in many of its local details: in the banishment and stocking of the forthright Kent as the figure of Justice in several moralities had been banished and stocked; in Lear's homily on charity on the heath; in his mock trial of his daughters and indictments of earthly justice; in his madness itself, for which there are precedents in pictorial and morality tradition if not in the play's actual sources; in the vision of redemption Lear superimposes on Cordelia at his reunion and again even amid the shambles of the closing scene. And given this wealth of archaic reference within the Lear action, the question arises: why does all that has just been said of the gross conventionality of the Gloucester action not apply to it as well? What is it that makes the one modern, mimetic, and tragic and the other conventional and pseudo-tragic?

What distinguishes the main plot from the subplot is not the extent to which but the manner in which these older

Plays Within Plays

conventions are employed. In fact, the opening scene of the Lear action is much closer to the moralities in its ritual stylization than is the more domesticated and fluent opening scene of the Gloucester action. For that opening scene, staged by Lear himself, proceeds from and reflects his absolute confidence in the sacred authority of his role of king and the perfect correspondence among the natural, moral, and linguistic orders that supports it. In the security of this traditional vision of the world, Lear cannot imagine any possible disjuncture between role and self, appearance and reality, "sentence and power," *signum* and *res*. Hence his surprise at Cordelia's unprogrammatic response of "nothing" and Kent's irreverent rejoinder to "see better." It is against this initial morality vision of sacred unity that Lear's descent into a more modern and secular perception of ironic discontinuity is defined. The movement of the Lear action away from a morality vision thus opposes and crosses that of the Gloucester action toward a morality vision. Of course Lear does not abandon his original mode of vision immediately or willingly. He clings to his former way of seeing himself and his world, curses his daughters with a residual belief in the magical efficacy of his word, and calls down "plagues that in the pendulous air / Hang fated o'er men's faults" (III.iv.65-66). But these invocations of a morality scheme of divine justice inherent in the natural order now ring increasingly hollow even to him and almost as he utters them: "What *is* the cause of thunder?" (III.iv. 146); "*Is* there any cause in nature that makes these hard hearts" (III.vi.75-76). The change that Lear undergoes in the course of his play is not a change from one moral state to another, such as from pride to charity, but a change away from self-definition in terms of moral categories altogether and toward a new sense of existential indeterminacy, the very opposite of Gloucester's change. For whereas Gloucester is increasingly allegorized within his action, Lear is increasingly humanized within his, though not in the sense of becoming more humane—witness his cruel greeting of the blinded Gloucester and his accusations of the reassembled court as "murderers, traitors all" (v.ii.271)—but in the sense of becoming more fully and merely human.

This is not to suggest that he does not continue to fall back on moral categories of self-definition, but that he recognizes them to be somehow inadequate even as he does so. His set speech on charity toward the "poor, naked wretches," (III.iv.28-36), for example, is right out of morality tradition and often cited as the beginning of Lear's moral re-education. But its imperative mood ("Take physic pomp") gives way by the end of the homily to the subjunctive and optative mood ("That thou may'st shake the superflux to them / and show the heavens more just"). Man, by practicing charity, can only hope to *show* the heavens more just; he cannot make them so. Similarly, his mad re-enactments of the forms of justice on the heath work to undermine the morality vision they represent. In that older drama, the satiric castigation of judicial corruption deals in such negative *exempla* as Lear offers, but only on the way to establishing a vision of true justice. Lear's recourse in his madness to this strain of morality rhetoric and imagery, however, works to strip away these social and religious legitimations to the emptiness and arbitrariness of the idea of justice itself, its fundamental disjuncture from a human nature that exists beneath or beyond moral and legal categories. Vice and guilt do not exist—"Die for adultery? No . . . None does offend" (IV.vi.165)—and neither does virtue and innocence: "Behold yond simp'ring dame . . . / The fitchew nor the soiled horse goes to 't / With a more riotous appetite" (IV.vi.108-112). Lear's view of the discrepancy between social forms and the human nature to which they are supposed to correspond is not at this point very far from Edmund's. The difference between them is not in moral outlook but in mimetic realization. Edmund holds his views lightly and complacently as a means of justifying himself and his actions; Lear comes to his reluctantly and

Plays Within Plays

painfully, after a lifetime of believing the opposite and against his present interests. Uniquely in the play, Lear's adoption of morality forms leads in each local instance and within his larger itinerary to a desperate fluctuation between his maddening perception of their inadequacy and a wishful retreat into the shelter they provide, however momentary.[8]

This breakdown of the morality forms by which the social order and the individual mind maintain their stability conditions not only Lear's madness in particular but Shake-

---

[8] In contrast to the easy volubility and willing credulity with which the characters of the subplot express and accept a moral for all occasions, Lear repeatedly displays a problematic relation to language itself almost from the beginning:

> Who is it that can tell me who I am?   (I.iv.236)

> I can scarce speak to thee. Thou'lt not believe
> With how depraved a quality—O Regan!   (II.iv.135-136)

> I will have such revenges on you both
> That all the world shall—I will do such things—
> What they are, yet I know not; but they shall be
> The terrors of the earth.   (II.iv.278-281)

> Howl, howl, howl, howl! O, you are men of stones:
> Had I your tongues and eyes, I'd use them so
> That heaven's vault should crack.   (V.iii.259-261)

These failures of speech, stammerings, outcries have no counterpart among the characters of the subplot, who are never at a loss for words. They point to the larger frustration and failure on the part of the principals—for Cordelia has foreseen the condition Lear discovers—to find an expressive form for feeling and action in the dramatic language of morality convention. By contrast, even Gloucester's "despair" is cogently expressed, and his own wavering between despair and faith is more a parody than a parallel of Lear's fluctuations. The "ill thoughts" he falls into after Edgar has indoctrinated him at Dover may correspond to Lear's own relapses into incoherence after his recuperation in the presence of Cordelia, but whereas Gloucester's wavering "'twixt joy and grief" is finally and happily resolved into joy as his heart bursts "smilingly," Lear's desperate fluctuation between morality and madness, as we shall see, goes too deep to achieve resolution.

Othello, King Lear, Antony and Cleopatra

spearean madness in general. For the roles and forms of morality convention, as we have repeatedly seen, are employed by Shakespeare's characters as a protection against the confusion of raw experience, a screen that selectively permits only that which can be made sense of within a predetermined order to reach the perceiving mind. But it is an inflexible screen, whose very rigidity renders it breakable, exposing the self to that which it can no longer process. It is only Shakespeare's protagonists—Hamlet, Othello, Lear, and Lady Macbeth—as characters whose role-playing is precarious and whose naked humanity is therefore most vulnerable, who are capable of true madness. Their foils are immune to madness, precisely because they are too thoroughly engrossed in their protective roles for an underlying self ever to be exposed in its naked frailty. Lear in his madness thus stands in contrast to Gloucester, who naively wishes he could go mad like Lear, mistaking madness for a protection against pain when it is in fact an exposure to it:

> The King is mad: how stiff is my vile sense,
> That I stand up, and have ingenious feeling
> Of my huge sorrows! Better I were distract:
> So should my thoughts be severed from my griefs,
> And woes by wrong imaginations lose
> The knowledge of themselves.
> (IV.vi.284-289)

Like his nakedness—to which it is the psychological correlative—Lear's madness also stands in contrast to Edgar's stagy and conventional madtalk of "sin" and "foul fiends." Edgar's "madness," as a role based upon a wholly traditional and external view of madness as demonic possession, is actually the antithesis of the true madness of Lear, since the latter arises from the breakdown of roles whereas the former is itself a role and therefore a protection against a maddening overperception. Like Edgar's mock-beggary, also deriving from a long tradition of moral iconography, his mock-madness is thus a shadow or parody of "the thing itself." It has the status of a sign emptied of its significance and divorced from the realities of nakedness and madness to which it refers, the absent referent in both cases being supplied by Lear. Within the universe of Shakespearean tragedy, madness is thus the opposite pole to morality, a vision of undifferentiated anarchy as opposed to one of a wholly mapped-out order.

The temptation at this point is to grant this vision of madness and absurdity a privileged status and equate it with the meaning of the play. But this tendency is only the modernist counterpart of the archeological tendency to do the same with the earlier vision of morality, and is no more valid. Because Lear's vision of madness is an inversion of his vision of morality, it remains dependent on it, derives its terms from it, and is capable of being turned back into it. This is exactly what happens, for neither morality nor madness constitutes a resting-point for Lear or Shakespeare, and both are left behind on the way to a truer, more austere mimesis. The fact is that Lear is able to maintain neither the complacent vision he shared with his society at the beginning nor the painful counter-vision he comes to in his alienation, though he tries desperately to maintain each in turn. For when he awakens from his ordeal in the presence of Cordelia, he would seem to have renounced his restless probing for a demystified and naturalistic explanation of his world. Cordelia seems to him "a soul in bliss," his madness the infernal or purgatorial punishment of "a wheel of fire," and his recovery nothing less than a resurrection wrought by this "spirit" to whom he now kneels and prays for benediction. Not only has Lear renounced his maddening effort to explain the world, to find out its true causes, he has renounced the world itself. In a spirit of *contemptus mundi*, he resigns all interest in the vindication he had formerly tried to call down on his persecutors, leaving them to "The good years" (v.iii.24) of plague and pestilence to be devoured in due course. He welcomes his life with Cordelia in prison with a religious joy, as if it were a posthumous or monastic existence removed from the mutability of earthly life. Indeed, Lear has awakened to find himself, like several converted morality protagonists before him, clothed in the fresh garments traditionally emblematic of an inner and spiritual reaccommodation.[9] Nowhere in the play is the return to an older morality vision so pure and complete, so strenuously and extravagantly reenacted—for we are still in the realm of histrionic recreation—as it is by Lear himself at the start of the final act. The play has all but reunited with its prototype, the wheel of interpretation come full circle.

If *King Lear* had ended here, we should still have had to say that Shakespeare has altered his sources significantly and, in so doing, achieved a representation of human depth and complexity quite beyond them and very much of the order of displaced Christian vision ascribed to the play by Bradley and Mack. But the final stage in the process of mimetic realization toward which the play moves consists in a still more radical putting into question of all prior visions—the vision of morality taken over from its sources and the counter-vision of madness introduced by Shakespeare alike—and that process has at this point only begun. For when Lear reenters shortly afterward with Cordelia in his arms, he no longer speaks in the recovered language of morality but in his earlier language of madness: "Howl, howl, howl, howl . . . / I know when one is dead and when one lives; / She's dead as earth" (v.iii.259-263). Yet by the end of this

---

[9] In the early morality, *Wisdom, Who Is Christ* (1425), for example, the regeneration of the protagonist Anima is marked by the following stage direction: "Here entrethe ANIMA, wyth the Fyve Wyttys goynge before, MYNDE on the on syde and WNDYRSTONDYNGE on the other syde and WYLL followyng, all in here fyrst clothynge. . . ." *The Macro Plays*, ed. Mark Eccles (E.E.T.S., Oxford, 1969), p. 149. On the significance of changes of costume in morality tradition, see T. W. Craik, *The Tudor Interlude: Stage, Costume, and Acting* (Leicester, 1967), pp. 49-92. Shakespeare calls attention to the fresh garments worn by his protagonists in similar moments of reunion and restoration in *Pericles* and *The Tempest*.

speech, he is calling for a looking-glass in the hope of life, which he then discovers in the very terms of Christian mystery: "This feather stirs; she lives. If it be so, / It is a chance which does redeem all sorrows / That ever I have felt" (v.iii. 267-269). Again, the play might well have ended here on this act of recuperation, however tentative, of the older vision. But it does not: "A plague upon you, murderers, traitors all! / I might have saved her. . . ." Or it could have ended soon afterward with Albany's assertion, however muted, of a restored justice of rewards and punishments. But it does not:

> And my poor fool is hanged: no, no, no life?
> Why should a dog, a horse, a rat have life,
> And thou no breath at all? Thou'lt come no more,
> Never, never, never, never, never.
> Pray you, undo this button. Thank you, sir.
> (v.iii.307-311)

Lear's fluctuation between the visions of morality and madness, meaning and absurdity, accommodation and disaccommodation becomes dizzying in its intensity. But still it seems to go on: "Do you see this? Look on her. Look, her lips, / Look there, look there." These parting lines might well be interpreted as another and final access of faith or delusion, yet they are themselves remarkably free of the mythologizations of either morality or madness, which have been only preludes to this moment and are now left behind. Lear's language and gesture now proceed not out of a convention of vision but out of a depth and fullness of feeling that is unquestionably "there" but unfathomable in its inwardness. His last lines merely point to a form that has also been "there" all along, though repeatedly misconstrued and overlooked, with no longer any attempt to define it. In the end, the play renounces its own mediations of morality and madness alike and redirects our attention to an undetermined reality that exists prior to and remains unavailable to both.

Othello, King Lear, Antony and Cleopatra

In the play that has come to be regarded as the definitive achievement of Shakespearean tragedy, Shakespeare has certainly not made things easy for us. For he leaves us in the end with not a choice of *either* morality and meaning *or* madness and absurdity, but more like an ultimatum of *neither* morality and meaning *nor* madness and absurdity, an ultimatum that becomes inescapable as a result of Lear's own strenuous and futile effort to remain within the realm of choice. Lear enacts in advance our own dilemma as interpreters, alternating between antithetical visions of experience, only to abandon both in favor of a pure and simple pointing to the thing itself. Interpreters of the play, like Albany, Kent, and Edgar within it, have been understandably reluctant to follow him into this state of aporia, of being completely at a loss, so peremptory is the human need to make sense of things, to find unity, coherence, resolution in the world of the text and the text of the world. Yet the aporia toward which not only *Lear*, but Shakespeare's other great tragedies, move represents the very negation of the possibility of unity, coherence, and resolution, of the accommodation that all our systems of explanation provide, be they pious or modernist, consoling or painful, older or newer. In his dizzying fluctuation between contradictory meanings, Lear reenacts the intense shifting between demystification and remystification of the self we saw in Othello's closing speech, which also ends with an act of pointing. We saw a similar movement in Hamlet's division between a last-gasp impulse to shape and tell his story—"O, I could tell you!"—and his equal and opposite impulse to repudiate self-mythologization altogether and return his play to the status of the most inexplicable dumb-show of all—"The rest is silence." Yet this very process of casting off inherited forms and imposed meanings to point to the thing itself only invites their reimposition. Like Horatio and Fortinbras, Cassio and Lodovico, Edgar and Albany, we feel we still can and must report Hamlet's story to the world and tell Othello and Lear who they are, even though they themselves, possessed of larger, tougher, and finer minds than we, have anticipated our attempt and thrown up their hands. The characters we *can* denote truly—Laertes, Cassio, Gloucester—do not ask to be told who they are, for such characters are content to remain within the defining forms that tradition provides and that society, with the wisdom of self-preservation, maintains as "true." Unlike his interpreters and his own choric commentators, however, Shakespeare never succumbs to the rhetorical pressure of the traditional forms he employs, to their built-in claim to have made sense of the world, but keeps them always in brackets and puts them ultimately into question. The Shakespearean text remains a step ahead of its critics, even at the very moment we think we have caught up with it.

These interpretive fluctuations between allegory and parody, remystification and demystification, morality and absurdity that arise from the structure of Shakespearean tragedy is carried even further—not in intensity but in pervasiveness—in *Antony and Cleopatra*. That this play creates an ambiguity of effect and response unprecedented even within Shakespeare's work is documented by a history of interpretation that wavers inconclusively between Egyptian and Roman viewpoints, and that usually feels compelled finally to side with one or the other position, however tentatively or tactfully. It is not immediately obvious, however, that the play's dominant ambiguity of effect arises from the juxtaposition of older and newer, allegorical and parodic, levels of action that we have been tracing as a constitutive feature of Shakespearean tragedy. On the contrary, does the play not present a pagan and classical world that manifestly exists outside native morality influences? Yet we need not even go as far back as the revenges of the Vice-like Aaron in *Titus Andronicus* to find Shakespeare changing his classical sources and subject-matter into the currency of his own popular dramatic tradition. The machinations of the Vice and the machinery of revenge are still clearly visible in Cassius' temptation of Brutus and the ap-

Othello, King Lear, Antony and Cleopatra

pearance of Caesar's ghost within *Julius Caesar*. In *Antony and Cleopatra*, it is the principals themselves who attempt to impose, in characteristic Shakespearean fashion, a morality structure upon themselves and their world, a structure closely analogous to the by now familiar one adopted by Hal in the earlier moral history, *1 Henry IV*.

For in *Antony and Cleopatra* too we see a worldly prince flanked by figures of vice and virtue and engaged in a movement toward redemption in which the former is reluctantly but inevitably cast off and the latter embraced. Indeed, the large structural contours of the play, as seen from the lovers', particularly Cleopatra's, viewpoint, could not be more transparently morality-derived. "O infinite virtue, com'st thou smiling from / The world's great snare uncaught" (IV.viii.17-18), she greets the temporarily victorious Antony, equating Caesar and the Romans with the temptations of the world, and herself and Egypt with a saving love. Obviously certain major adjustments and displacements have already been worked on the older vision of transcendence to enable the lovers to adopt it as their own. For one thing, the virtues of love and faith incarnated and preached by Cleopatra are hardly those of traditional Christian allegory; in her carnality and selfishness, she might well be said to embody the very opposite of Christian virtue, yet the play, as even its most Roman commentators have often pointed out, systematically transvalues her vices into virtues, for they partake of a quality of transcendence that is repeatedly said to be sacred and divine. Nor is the "salvation" the lovers finally see their way clear to in the end the traditional Christian one of the moralities. Their "marriage" is a shared figure of speech; their "afterlife" in a pastoral underworld an imaginative projection; Antony's apotheosis takes the form of the visual pun of being raised aloft on creaking pulleys. And all this is achieved by the most un-Christian means of a double suicide. Obviously the allegorical model to which the lovers would assimilate themselves and their experience is already something of a parody.

Plays Within Plays

If this neo- or pseudo-morality structure were the only one, or even the major one, employed within the play, the effect would certainly be highly ambiguous, given the relatively loose fit and the amount of adjustment necessary between the present action and the prior model. But this initial ambiguity is increased almost geometrically by virtue of the fact that juxtaposed against the model employed by the lovers is another competing model of experience. For the Romans have adopted for their own purposes of self-mythologization the heroic model of the renaissance epic.[10] Seen from within that literary convention, Cleopatra is no longer a figure of the saving power of love and grace, however displaced or redefined, but a figure of deceit and corruption, seducing the hero from his true mission of self-realization through heroic conquest. Cleopatra is assigned, through the Romans' language and imagery, a place within a long line of emasculating and hypererotic *femmes fatales*, stretching from the Venus, Omphale, Circe, and Dido of classical tradition to the Armida, Duessa, and Acrasia of more recent renaissance epics. Antony becomes the enfeebled descendant of Hercules figuratively as well as genealogically, and Octavius becomes the surviving heir to the line of antique virtue. This is the screen through which all the Romans, including Antony himself much of the time, view the experience of the play, from Philo's opening speech announcing "The triple pillar of the world transformed / Into a strumpet's fool" to Octavius' closing description of Cleopatra looking "As she would catch another Antony / In her strong toil of grace." Even Enobarbus' depiction of Cleopatra on Cydnus, usually quoted in support of her claim to transcendence, falls squarely within this renaissance epic and pictorial tradition in its emphasis on fine excess and analogy with the sexually threatening Venus. Of course this high epic tradition that the Romans invoke and culti-

[10] The renaissance epic and pictorial analogues of the play are discussed in some detail by Janet Adelman, *The Common Liar* (New Haven, 1973), pp. 53-101.

vate throughout the play contains its own suggestion of parody. The latter-day embodiment of Herculean virtue, "scarce-bearded Caesar," has come down in the world considerably from his heroic antecedents, refusing on pragmatic grounds Antony's anachronistic challenge to single combat, and exhibiting throughout a politician's preference for the duplicities of the fox over the directness of the Nemean lion. Such ironies should at least prevent us from privileging the Roman view of things, as truer or closer to "reality," over that of the lovers. Both are equally fictive and equally at variance with their implied prototypes.

If these rival constructs were allowed to remain impenetrable to one another while alternately presenting contradictory images of character and action, the overall effect would be one not of ambiguity and ambivalence but of schizophrenia or solipsism, as it is in the closing scenes of *Troilus and Cressida*. But in *Antony and Cleopatra*, as Octavius' phrase "strong toil of grace" suggests, there is considerable interpenetration between its two rival constructs as they engage each other in a dialectic of mutual demystification. For each enables us to see the weakness or inadequacy of the other as a model of conduct. It is the Roman vision of the lovers as a pair of degenerate hedonists that reveals, against their own vision of themselves, how lacking in anything like a social morality is the neo-morality they stage. If their vision were generally adopted, there could not be a society at all, much less an empire. Conversely, it is the lovers' vision of the Romans as a gang of petty worldlings that reveals, against their own self-mythologization, how far short of their epic forbears these squabbling and treacherous Romans fall. Yet these rival constructs are simultaneously engaged in a dialectic of mutual remystification. By adopting an epic model, however short of its ideal of heroic magnanimity they themselves fall, the Romans enable us to see that the lovers' reconstituted virtue approaches this very epic norm. Similarly, the lovers' morality vision, though they have emptied it of conventional morality, enables us to

Plays Within Plays

see that this older-style morality, as embodied by Fulvia and Octavia, is the very pillar on which the Roman social order rests. Both older visions might actually seem to have survived their mutual conflict in Caesar's closing speech: "No grave upon the earth shall clip in 't / A pair so famous." Here the Romans' historical and rhetorical model of epic glory ("A pair so *famous*") has apparently been reconciled with the lovers' model of saving passion ("No grave shall *clip* . . ."), since the spokesman of the former has adopted the vocabulary of the latter. The impression of reconciliation is only momentary, however, since Caesar's speech goes on to glorify himself and Rome in terms of their *triumph over* the lovers, whose story is "No less in pity than his glory which / Brought them to be lamented." Caesar does not so much adopt their language as commandeer it as the spoils of victory. Of course this is no more than what Antony and Cleopatra have already done in claiming to have validated their own transcendent vision of passion and "marriage" by committing suicide "in the high Roman manner." The apparent reconciliation of contending models in the end gives way to a continuing and endless process of demystification and remystification of older models we have seen to be characteristic of Shakespearean tragedy.

Though this interaction of older conventions does begin to imply or triangulate the reality of the lovers and their experience, it cannot, for all its richness and complexity, finally contain and comprehend those realities. We can believe that the lovers have indeed succeeded in defining themselves and validating their love in the terms they insist upon, if we wish, but to do so is to regard their and Shakespeare's art as a kind of displaced religion and to disregard Shakespeare's presentation of it as merely art.[11] When Cleo-

---

[11] Janet Adelman's discerning analysis of the lovers' imaginative and rhetorical strategies, for example, is finally in the service of privileging their vision as an act of faith and an object of belief: "If we come to believe in the assertions of the poetry, it is, I think, precisely because they are so unbelievable. One of the tricks of the human imagi-

patra, for example, at the play's most intense moment of theatrical self-consciousness imagines "Some squeaking Cleopatra boy my greatness / In the posture of a whore" (v.ii.214-215), she appropriates the terms of the Roman vision of her only to disclaim them. She is not, she implies, this caricature of a whore the Romans would make her out to be. She parodies their parody, deconstructs their construct of disapproval and doubt, rendering it null and void. This opens up imaginative space for her own "immortal longings" to express themselves, for her to become once again and once and for all an allegorical being of "fire and air, / My baser elements I give to baser life." But how can we simply lay aside our awareness that her greatness *is* being "boyed" and perhaps even "squeaked" in something very like the posture of a whore by the boy-actor playing her, at least in Elizabethan production, and at the very moment such artistic mockery is disclaimed and supposedly transcended to make way for authentic reality? Or when Antony asserts "I am Antony still," there is no more basis for identifying him with the walking hyperbole that defines Antony within Cleopatra's vision than with the reeling reduction of a "strumpet's fool" that defines him within the Romans'. The play cannot finally bring moral resolution out of what remains a double image, but it is precisely in its moral irresolution that its mimetic fidelity consists. The failure of their efforts toward self-deification is what defines them in their exemplary humanity.

Like Shakespeare's earlier tragedies, *Antony and Cleopatra* can finally only point toward, but cannot present, a

---

nation is that an appeal to the rationally possible is not always the most effective means of insuring belief: occasionally an appeal to the impossible, an appeal to doubt, works wonders. *Antony and Cleopatra* embodies in its structure the paradox of faith: the exercise of faith is necessary only when our reason dictates doubt." *The Common Liar*, pp. 110-111. This implicit theologization of the play in response to the allegorical element in its own structure parallels that performed by Bradley and Mack on *King Lear*.

Plays Within Plays

stable selfhood that resides beneath the roles adapted from the repertory of literary and dramatic tradition, a reality that does not vary like the shore of the great world or dislimn like the cloud-rack. But this reality cannot exist as such within the play, and remains just beyond the reach, though not the reference, of its own art. Unlike *Lear* and the earlier tragedies, however, *Antony and Cleopatra* does not end in intense aporia, but only because the lovers, and the Romans, accept as true the rhetoric of their own models, as Lear and the other tragic heroes can never quite do. In this respect, the play moves toward the joyful reunion with its implied models that characterizes Shakespearean comedy and romance rather than toward the unsettling divergence that characterizes Shakespearean tragedy. This feeling may well be what moved A. C. Bradley to remark that "for a tragedy it is not painful" and what has led many others to think of the play as somehow different from the four great tragedies and to be discussed in different terms.[12] But the fact remains that Shakespeare has at every point made it possible to resist this movement of the play toward convergence with either or both its inscribed models, if only because those models are mutually contradictory to the end, which is also what finally maintains the play within the mode of tragedy. Sidney's fundamental insight that "the poet never lieth because he nothing affirmeth" fits no poet better than the Shakespeare of the tragedies, including the Shakespeare of *Antony and Cleopatra*.

The interplay of rival visions we have seen in *Antony and Cleopatra* suggests a further and necessary adjustment to the interpretive model we have constructed from within the earlier tragedies and a further reason why this play exists in our minds somewhat apart from them. Though *Antony* employs a model not essentially different from those within *Othello* and *Lear*, it also employs another and very different one. It is obvious from *Antony* that Shakespeare

[12] *Oxford Lectures on Poetry* (Bloomington, 1961), p. 282.

is fully capable of subsuming within his tragedies older models other than or in addition to those drawn from the native tradition of religious drama, with a resulting change of tone and effect. The Roman tragedies are the most obvious examples. The unusually austere atmosphere of *Coriolanus* results from its hero's own relentless and exclusive classicism in patterning himself after previous epic heroes. His angry withdrawal from his society and reluctant reconciliation to it follow closely upon the pattern of Achilles' heroic career. (Plutarch twice draws parallels to Achilles' anger in his *Life of Coriolanus*.) Locked inside the gates of the enemy town and cut off from his own troops, Coriolanus welcomes this occasion for undivided glory in the spirit of another Achillean figure from the Roman past, the Turnus of the ninth book of the *Aeneid*, also a caricature of martial bloodlust and an unwitting opponent of Rome's unfolding destiny. Absorbed in the idea of epic heroism and *virtus* as he is, Coriolanus refuses to acknowledge that he is playing anything like a role and prides himself on the antipathy to role-playing of "my disposition" and "mine own truth." Yet the histrionic side of his nature, though hidden to him, is highlighted by the rest of the cast, who portray him as "painted," "mantled," and "masqued" in blood, the element of his chief epic predecessor. Even off the battlefield, he is at his most Achillean when he acquiesces to his mother's supplications to withdraw his troops. In the course of that scene, Coriolanus re-enacts both Achilles' rejection of the Greek embassy in book nine and Achilles' relenting to Priam in book twenty-four of the *Iliad*, foreseeing his imminent death and softening in filial piety as Achilles had before him. Coriolanus' tragedy proceeds not from his inability to play a role but from his persistence in playing an outmoded and inappropriate role, his refusal, as Volumnia says, to "perform a part / Thou hast not done before" (III.ii.109-110). By remaining within a heroic precedent that is essentially Homeric, Coriolanus pits himself against what one critic has termed "the complexities and necessary compromises of the Roman-Jacobean political world."[13] In this tragic opposition Shakespeare models his play upon Virgil, who is repeatedly evoked through the name of the hero's wife, and who is the most palpable influence on the play's sinewy verse.

Nor do the models Shakespeare subsumes within his tragedies have to be classical when they are not native. In *Romeo and Juliet*, to glance briefly at a final example, the convention is Petrarchan. The sonnet and its variants inform the choruses of the first two acts, Romeo's descriptions of his love for Rosaline (1.i.174-187; 1.ii.91-102), Lady Capulet's praise of Paris (1.ii.81-94), and the lovers' first encounter at the banquet (1.v.95-108). Shakespeare's task as a dramatist might indeed be said to parallel Romeo and Juliet's as lovers: to re-create the Petrarchan language of love, which might well have seemed always the same and empty of real content even in 1595, into a language of authenticity.[14] To this end, Romeo's highly rhetorical love for Rosaline, which the Friar says "did read by rote," and the equally bookish Paris' love for Juliet serve as conventional foils, against which a more authentic language and love is seen to originate. The chorus falls away, rhyme becomes scarce, and what had been mere figures of speech in Romeo's conventional account of his love for Rosaline—"brawling love," "loving hate," "cold fire," "still-waking sleep"—become facts of life and death with Juliet, who takes Romeo from the balcony-scene onward "at thy word." The integrity of sign and sense, which had been put asunder for purposes of wit in Petrarchan tradition, is momentarily put back together in their death at the tomb of the Capulets. This mimetic realization of prior convention is of course fleeting,

---

[13] The depth and pervasiveness of classical influence on *Coriolanus* is suggestively and richly, if unsystematically, studied by Reuben A. Brower, *Hero and Saint: Shakespeare and the Graeco-Roman Heroic Tradition* (Oxford, 1971), pp. 354-381.

[14] See Leslie Brisman, " 'At Thy Word': A Reading of *Romeo and Juliet*," *MMLA*, 8 (1975), pp. 21-31.

Othello, King Lear, Antony and Cleopatra

since its condition is death, and sign is again tragically disjoined from sense in the choric recapitulations offered at the end by Friar Lawrence and the Prince. Their love passes back into art, into mere sign, in the form of a golden statue to be erected in the town square of Verona. As in the case of *Coriolanus*, the particular convention inscribed within *Romeo and Juliet* is non-native, nonreligious, and even nondramatic. But its function as a mimetic point of reference and historical point of departure to set off Shakespeare's own play is not essentially different from that of the native tradition of religious drama within the major tragedies.

Indeed, if we were to go on to apply *to* the tragedies the mimetic principle we have derived *from* them, it would be those tragedies that are not based on native models which actually help to define by contrast the distinctive character of those that are. *Hamlet*, *Othello*, *King Lear*, and *Macbeth* have become virtually synonymous with "Shakespearean tragedy," not simply because of their artistic superiority, but because of the particular dramatic models these plays have in common with one another, and the similarities of structure and atmosphere that result. Of course Shakespeare employs models other than those drawn from native religious drama in his tragedies, even within the major tragedies. The convention of Petrarchanism, for example, is enlisted by Othello in his effort to define himself and by his foil, Cassio. Yet no critic to my knowledge has suggested that *Othello* has more in common with *Romeo and Juliet* than with *Hamlet* or *Lear*, even though it shares with *Romeo* and not with *Hamlet* or *Lear* not only its use of the sonnet convention but its thematic content of love and its renaissance Italian setting.[15] It is their common recourse to

[15] It may well be precisely these elements that led Bradley to set *Othello* somewhat apart from the three other great tragedies. He points out that it is "a drama of modern life" and that "If . . . we feel it to occupy a place in our minds a little lower than the other three (and I believe this feeling, though not general, is not rare), the reason lies

Plays Within Plays

native religious models that transcends these differences of setting and theme, enables—even encourages—us to discuss them as a group, and makes them definitive of what we think of as "Shakespearean tragedy" in the first place. Obviously the study of available tradition as the enabling condition of Shakespeare's art could lead in many directions, for the fact that Shakespeare is a renaissance poet in a simply historical or chronological sense means that a wide range of literary and dramatic traditions are open to him. But in the more strictly literary-historical sense we have been exploring, his status as a renaissance poet means that he is a medieval and modern poet simultaneously; and so, the place to begin the study of his relation to available tradition is with the particular tradition which defines that unique identity in its full complexity, which can fairly be said to be predominant, normative, and characteristic, and which therefore has a special claim on our attention.[16] For

---

not here but in another characteristic, to which I have already referred,—the comparative confinement of the imaginative atmosphere." *Shakespearean Tragedy*, pp. 148, 151.

[16] The present study is obviously based on an understanding of what constitutes Shakespeare's "sources" rather different from the one commonly assumed. In general, the study of his sources is either too narrowly or too diffusely conceived. On the one hand, it consists of collecting, editing, and comparing the specific works that provide Shakespeare with his plots and with certain scenic or verbal details; on the other, of general discussions of the diverse literary and dramatic conventions and *topoi* reflected in his work as well as that of other renaissance poets and playwrights, discussions such as Madeleine Doran's *Endeavors of Art* (Madison, 1954) or Rosalie Colie's *Shakespeare's Living Art* (Princeton, 1974). What I have been calling his imaginative models, particularly those drawn from native dramatic tradition, are still largely ignored, or are at least not given intensive study. Though they sometimes coincide with his "sources," as in the main plot of *Lear*, and are certainly among the conventions available to any Elizabethan dramatist, these models are of especial interest in determining Shakespeare's distinctive relation to his past, because they usually condition the way he employs his other sources and conventions, as in the subplot of *Lear*.

Othello, King Lear, Antony and Cleopatra

even when they are not aware of the presence of these models behind and within his work, and even when they fail to recognize his radical revision of them, critics of Shakespeare's great tragedies have always responded to the special urgency of tone and universality of theme that are themselves traceable to the morality tradition present within these plays and that distinguish them from even Shakespeare's other tragedies. All of which brings us to the last of the four great tragedies, *Macbeth*.

CHAPTER 4

A Painted Devil: *Macbeth*

> 'Tis the eye of childhood
> That fears a painted devil.
> —*Macbeth,* ii.ii.53-54

THE LAST of Shakespeare's major tragedies to depend primarily on a native tradition of religious drama is also the most widely and seriously misunderstood in its relation to it. Indeed, *Macbeth* might well appear to be an exception to the principle of Shakespearean revision we have educed from the earlier tragedies. In those plays, the effect of mimetic naturalization over and above the older models contained within them had been achieved precisely by revealing the moral oversimplification of those models, in sum, by problematizing them. But *Macbeth* is unique among the major tragedies in having generated nothing like the central and recurrent problems that have shaped interpretation of *Hamlet, Othello, King Lear,* and even *Antony and Cleopatra.* Certain aspects of the play have of course received more than their share of attention and are continuing matters of debate: the status of its witches and of witchcraft; its topical relation to James I; the authorship of the Hecate scenes, yet these are more pre-critical problems of background and provenance than critical problems as such. For *Macbeth,* as Shakespeare's one "tragedy of damnation," is so widely acknowledged to exist within a relatively familiar dramatic tradition, that critical response to the play has become almost a matter of reflex in assimilating the play to it. This would seem to contradict the argument so far advanced that Shakespearean tragedy is fundamentally and finally unassimilable to its models, and

Macbeth

that this unassimilability is what underlies and generates their problematic status and realistic effect in the first place. At the risk of bringing chaos into order by discovering problems where none have existed, I want now to re-examine the relation between *Macbeth* and its inscribed models in the light of the previous discussion. It may turn out that those models are not quite the ones usually said to lie behind the play, and its relation to them not the clear and settled congruity that it is generally thought to be.

The tradition within which Macbeth is almost universally interpreted is that of orthodox Christian tragedy, the characteristic features of which are already well developed as early as Bocaccio and Lydgate and are familiar to all students of medieval and renaissance literature. It typically presents the fall of a man who may be basically or originally good but is always corruptible through the temptations of the world and his own pride or ambition. This action occurs against the structure of a fundamentally ordered and benevolent universe, which is finally self-restorative despite the evil and chaos temporarily unleashed within it, since crime will out and sin is always repaid. Of course the point in this essentially didactic genre is to illustrate the wages of human wrong-doing and the inexorability of divine purpose. That *Macbeth*, with its malign forces of temptation embodied in the witches, its vacillating but increasingly callous protagonist, and its restorative movement in the figures of Malcolm and Macduff, has affinities with this tradition is obvious and undeniable. The moral pattern of Shakespeare's play is not essentially different from that set forth in Boccaccio and Lydgate, and there is no lack of more immediate versions of it with which Shakespeare would have been well acquainted. He had drawn on *A Mirror for Magistrates* in previous histories and tragedies; several sixteenth-century moralities deal with the same theme; and the same pattern, though without political overtones, informs *Dr. Faustus*, a play with which *Macbeth* is often compared. Shakespeare's own early Marlovian monodrama, *Richard*

A Painted Devil

III, falls squarely within this tradition of Christian tragedy, and its similarities with *Macbeth* were pointed out as far back as the eighteenth century.

Yet there is another dramatic tradition at work within *Macbeth* or, more accurately, a sub-genre of this same tradition, that is at once much older than these examples and more immediately and concretely present within the play. For here, as in *Hamlet*, Shakespeare allows the primary model for his own action to remain at least partly in view. We have already seen how the cry of the elder Hamlet's ghost to "remember me" is more than a reminder to his son to avenge his death; it simultaneously conjures up the older mode of being and acting which would make revenge possible, which the action of *Hamlet* at once repeats and supersedes, and which points with all the intentionality and ambiguity of any sign toward the heart of the play's meaning. In *Macbeth*, too, the persistence of an older dramatic mode within the world of Shakespeare's play is no less explicitly recalled. Though there are many places in *Macbeth* that could serve as an entry into this older world, the two modern scholars who have consciously perceived its existence have both entered it through, so to speak, its front door, the "hell-gate" of Inverness with its attendant "devil-porter." For here too the purpose of the porter's request, "I pray you remember the porter" (II.iii.22), is more than to extract a tip from Macduff whom he has just admitted. The reference of his remark is ambiguous, as Glynne Wickham observes, "for it can be addressed by the actor both to Macduff and to the audience. As in the porter's dream, it is in two worlds at once; that of Macbeth's castle and that of another scene from another play which has just been recalled for the audience and which the author wants them to remember."[1]

---

[1] *Shakespeare's Dramatic Heritage* (New York, 1969), p. 222. Wickham's discussion of the influence of the cycle plays on *Macbeth* is reprinted in part from *Shakespeare Survey 19*, ed. Kenneth Muir (Cambridge, 1966), pp. 68-74. See also John B. Harcourt, "I Pray You, Remember the Porter," *Shakespeare Quarterly*, XII (1961), 393-402.

Macbeth

That other play, which Wickham advances as Shakespeare's "model for the particular form in which he chose to cast Act II, scene iii, of *Macbeth*, and possibly for the play as a whole,"[2] is *The Harrowing of Hell* in the medieval English mystery cycles. Derived from the apocryphal *Gospel of Nicodemus* and adapted in two of the oldest rituals of the Roman Catholic liturgy, it is enacted in all of the extant cycles, though details of staging and dialogue differ from one to another. Between his crucifixion and resurrection, Christ comes to hell (represented as a castle on the medieval stage) and demands of Lucifer the release of the souls of the prophets and patriarchs. In all versions, the arrival of Christ is heralded by strange noises in the air and thunderous knocking at the castle gates. In the York and Towneley plays, the gate of hell has a porter appropriately named Rybald, a comic devil who breaks the news to Beelzebub of Christ's arrival and questions David and Christ himself as to his identity. Finally, Jesus breaks down the gate of hell, routs the resisting devils and, after a debate with Satan, who tries to deny the prophecies of his godhead, releases the prophets amid prayers and rejoicing. The Coventry version of the playlet, the one that Shakespeare is almost certain to have seen, is not extant, but there is no reason to think it was substantially different from the other versions. In fact, the Pardoner in John Heywood's *The Foure PP* (1529?), is described as having been on easy terms with "the devyll that kept the gate," since he had "oft in the play of Corpus Christi . . . played the devyll at Coventry," and is himself addressed as "Good mayster porter."[3] With its castle setting, bumbling porter named Rybald, "*Clamor vel sonitus materialis magnus*"[4] in the depth of night, and background of prophecy, the cyclic play of the Harrowing of Hell would have been easily evoked by the business of *Macbeth*, II,iii in the minds of many in Shakespeare's audience

[2] Wickham, p. 215.

[3] J. M. Manly, ed., *Specimens of the Pre-Shakespearean Drama* (Boston, 1900), vol. I, p. 510.

[4] *The Chester Plays, Part II* (E.E.T.S., London, 1959), p. 323.

A Painted Devil

who still remembered the porter. Moreover, the memory of the old play would strongly foreshadow the outcome of *Macbeth* as well, since Christ's entry into and deliverance of the castle of hell also looks forward to Macduff's second entry into Macbeth's castle and triumph over the demonic Macbeth at the end of the play.

Though prefiguring the didactic superplot or counterplot of Macduff's liberation of Scotland and defeat of Macbeth, however, *The Harrowing of Hell* has little direct bearing on the main or central action of Macbeth's personal destiny within the play, aside from rather broadly associating him with Beelzebub or Satan. But there is another play, or rather pair of plays, in the mystery cycles that supply what *The Harrowing of Hell* leaves out in the action of *Macbeth*, namely *The Visit of the Magi* and *The Massacre of the Innocents*. The cycles are more varied in their dramatization of these episodes from St. Matthew than they are in the case of the deliverance from hell, particularly as to the outcome of the massacre, but all share certain elements that bear directly on Macbeth's career. In all of them, three wise men come to pay homage to a king born in Israel and descended from David, the prophecies of whose birth they rehearse to Herod. Outraged at these prophecies of a king not descended from him, which are confirmed by his own Biblical interpreters, Herod plans to murder the magi and all the children of Israel. The magi escape, warned by an angel, whereupon Herod sends his soldiers out to exterminate his rival, who also escapes into Egypt. The outcome of Herod's brutality—the murders are carried out on stage amid the pleas and lamentation of the mothers—though different in each version, is in all cases heavy with dramatic irony. The Towneley play, for example, concludes with a self-deluded Herod proclaiming that "Now in pease may I stand / I thank the Mahowne!"[5] In the York and Coventry versions, the irony is more explicit, as the soldiers of the former admit under questioning that they are not sure

[5] *The Towneley Plays* (E.E.T.S., London, 1966), p. 180.

Macbeth

whether Jesus was among the "brats" they have murdered, and in the latter a Messenger informs Herod that "All thy dedis ys cum to noght; / This chyld ys gone in-to Eygipte to dwell."[6] In the Chester play, Herod's own son is murdered by his soldiers while in the care of one of the women. When told the news, Herod dies in a paroxysm of rage and is carried off to hell by devils. Even more pointed and ironic is the *Ludus Coventriae* version, in which Herod stages a feast to celebrate the successful execution of his plan to consolidate his reign and succession. Its mirth and minstrelsy are interrupted with the stage-direction, "*Hic dum* [the minstrels] *buccinant mors interficiat herodem et duos milites subito et diabolus recipiat eos.*" While the devil drags Herod away, the spectral figure of Death, "nakyd and pore of array" closes the play with the inevitable moral: "I come sodeynly with-in a stownde / me with-stande may no castle / my jurnay wyl I spede."[7]

The appearance of death at Herod's feast cannot help but recall the appearance of Banquo's ghost at Macbeth's feast. For even though this motif of death at the feast of life occurs only in this one version of the Herod plays, it is a medieval topos which must have been available to Shakespeare from other dramatic or pictorial sources, if not from this particular play, since he had already employed it in Fortinbras' image at the end of *Hamlet*:

> O proud Death,
> What feast is toward in thine eternal cell,
> That thou so many princes at a shot
> So bloodily hast struck?
>
> (v.ii.353-356)

Indeed, the influence of the medieval cycles on *Macbeth* is not confined to the pair of plays already discussed but can

---

[6] *Two Coventry Corpus Christi Plays*, ed. Hardin Craig (E.E.T.S., London, 1957), p. 31.

[7] *Ludus Coventriae or The Plaie Called Corpus Christi*, ed. K. S. Block (E.E.T.S., London, 1922), pp. 176-177.

A Painted Devil

be traced to other plays within the same cycles. Shakespeare's choric trio of witches, for example, are anticipated not only by the three kings in *The Adoration of the Magi*, but by the three shepherds and the three prophets in the play that precedes it in the Coventry and other cycles, *The Adoration of the Shepherds*. There, both the shepherds and the prophets are granted foreknowledge of Christ's birth, both discuss his prophesied kingship, and in the Chester version, both employ a form of paradoxical salutation similar to that of Shakespeare's witches:

> *Primus Pastor.* Haile, King of heaven so hy, born in a Cribbe . . . !
> *Secundus Pastor.* Haile the, Emperour of hell, and of heaven als . . . !
> *Tertius Pastor.* Haile, prynce withouthen peere, that mankind shall releeve . . . ![8]

Moreover, prophecies of the birth of a potentially subversive child trouble not only Herod, but both Pharaoh and Caesar Augustus before him in the Towneley cycle. Both follow the same, self-defeating course of attempting to defy the prophecies through promiscuous slaughter. Certain details of the Towneley play of Pharaoh may even find their way, from this or other versions of the story, into some of Macbeth's most famous language and imagery. His miraculous lines on how "this my hand / Will rather the multitudinous seas incarnadine, / Making the green one red" (II.ii.60-62) may well have their humble beginning in the reported outcome of Pharaoh's equivocations with Moses, the first of Egypt's plagues:

> Syr, the Waters that were ordand
> for men and bestis foyde,
> Thrugh outt all egypt land,
> ar turnyd into reede-bloyde.[9]

---

[8] *The Chester Plays, Part I* (E.E.T.S., London, 1926), p. 155-156.
[9] *The Towneley Plays*, p. 73.

Macbeth

Or Macbeth's anguished outcry, "O, full of scorpions is my mind, dear wife!" (III.i.36) may echo the same soldier's account of the third plague while internalizing it: "Greatte mystis [of gnats], sir, there is both morn and noyn, / byte us full bytterly."[10] Even the plague of darkness may contain the hint for the dominant imagery of Shakespeare's play. It is not my intention to press these parallels as literal "sources," but it is important to recognize the close affinities of *Macbeth* with a series of Biblical tyrant plays, all repeating essentially the same story, each of whose protagonists—Satan, Pharaoh, Caesar, Herod—is a type of tyranny within a providential scheme of history. The apparently innocent request to "remember the porter" opens up an historical context for *Macbeth* that we have only begun to explore.

What, then, is the significance of these largely neglected models as they are deliberately recalled within Shakespeare's play? Glynne Wickham sums up their contribution to *Macbeth* as follows:

> The essentials that he drew from the play [of Herod] are the poisoning of a tyrant's peace of mind by the prophecy of a rival destined to eclipse him, the attempt to forestall that prophecy by the hiring of assassins to murder all potential rivals and the final overthrow and damnation of the tyrant. . . . Like Herod with the Magi, Macbeth adopts a twofold plan. He aims first at Banquo and Fleance; and, when this plan miscarries, he extends his net to cover all potential rivals and strikes down Lady Macduff and her children. The last twenty lines of this scene are imbued with the sharpest possible verbal, visual and emotional echoes of the horrific scene in Bethlehem. Young Seward's image of Macbeth as both tyrant and devil in Act v, scene vii, recalls the drunken devil-porter of Act II, scene iii, and thereby the two complementary images of the religious stage, Herod the tyrant and the Harrowing of Hell, are linked to one another in com-

---

[10] *The Towneley Plays*, p. 73.

A Painted Devil

pressed form to provide the thematic sub-text of this Scottish tragedy. Pride and ambition breed tyranny: tyranny breeds violence, a child born of fear and power: but tyrants are by their very nature Lucifer's children and not God's, and as such they are damned. As Christ harrowed Hell and released Adam from Satan's dominion, so afflicted subjects of mortal tyranny will find a champion who will release them from fear and bondage. This Macduff does for Scotland."[11]

The passage is worth quoting at such length because it so accurately reflects not only the indisputable elements Shakespeare takes over in *Macbeth* from the medieval tyrant plays but the doctrinal message those plays were designed to illustrate and inculcate, a moral orientation that critics much less conscious of dramatic traditions and much more "modern" and secular in outlook than Wickham also find in *Macbeth*. But to assimilate the meaning of *Macbeth* to that of its medieval models, as Wickham and most other critics of the play more or less explicitly do, is not only to make Shakespeare's play less interesting than it is but to make it say something it does not say. Such an interpretive stance is based on a misunderstanding of the way any truly great writer uses his sources and models, as well as the way Shakespeare used his own in this play.

For the resemblances of plot structure, characterization, even language between *Macbeth* and the medieval cycle plays cannot simply be ascribed to a pious attitude and a parallel intent on Shakespeare's part in relation to his models. All these resemblances arise in the first place as a result of the efforts of characters within the work to turn the action in which they are involved toward or even into a certain kind of older action, to recreate their experience in the image of certain precedents for their own purposes, purposes which cannot be immediately identified with the author's and which the play as a whole may not ratify. We have already seen this impulse at play within *Hamlet* and

[11] Wickham, pp. 230-231.

Macbeth

the previous tragedies, where Hamlet, Othello, and Lear all attempt and fail to turn the action into a version of the morality play, and it is no less present and pervasive in *Macbeth*, though here the particular medieval convention involved is a somewhat different one. For from the inception of the Scottish counterplot, Malcolm, Macduff, and the others are given to recreating present history in terms of medieval dramatic conventions. In Malcolm's depiction of him during the interlude at the English court, for example, Edward the Confessor is presented not as an historical monarch but as a type of royal saintliness, the dispenser of "The healing benediction" and possessor of "a heavenly gift of prophecy" (IV.iii.156-158). In contrast to the England blessed with such a king, Scotland has become, in Ross's account, a place "Where sighs and groans, and shrieks that rent the air, / Are made, not marked; where violent sorrow seems / A modern ecstasy" (IV.iii.168-170), that is, a hell on earth that cries out for the harrowing. Its ruler becomes, in Macduff's words, "Devilish Macbeth," "this fiend of Scotland" than whom "Not in the legions / Of horrid hell can come a devil more damned" (IV.iii.55-56). In the same highly stylized and archaic vein, Malcolm proceeds to characterize himself, first as a walking abstract and brief chronicle of vices exceeding even those of the collective portrait of Macbeth, and then as an equally abstract model of virtue allied to Edward the Confessor. To seek some naturalistic basis for his highly abstract "testing" of Macduff is futile, for like Hamlet's "portrait-test," its rhetorical and theatrical overdetermination will always be in excess of any personal motive that can be offered in so far as it is inspired by old plays rather than present feeling. Malcolm, like Hamlet, must go out of his way to abstract and depersonalize himself and his world as a necessary prelude to the scenario of redress being contemplated. He and his fellows must remake Scottish history into moral allegory, thereby legitimating themselves and their historical cause by assimilating them to an absolute and timeless struggle of good against evil. Malcolm and his party must, in sum,

A Painted Devil

represent themselves and their world, in precisely the terms of the play's medieval models, that is, in the name of all that is holy.

This effort to abstract themselves to older and purer roles, however, is not the exclusive prerogative of the angelic party of Malcolm and his followers and not confined to the Scottish superplot. A complementary but antithetical project is already underway near the beginning of the play in Lady Macbeth's attempt to become one with a demonic role:

> Come, you spirits
> That tend on mortal thoughts, unsex me here,
> And fill me from the crown to the toe top-full
> Of direst cruelty. Make thick my blood;
> Stop up th' access and passage to remorse,
> That no compunctious visitings of nature
> Shake my fell purpose....
>
> (I.v.38-44)

Her terrible soliloquy is appropriately cast in the language of the tiring room, as if its speaker were an actress beckoning attendants to costume her and make her up for the part she is about to perform, to "unsex" and depersonalize her into yet a fourth weird sister, even to dehumanize her into the "fiend-like" creature that Malcolm styles her at the end. All her efforts are bent toward making herself into a creature who trades lightly, even whimsically, in evil, and if her soliloquy echoes something of the incantatory tone of the witches' speeches, her utterances surrounding the murder reproduce something of their levity:

> Give me the daggers. The sleeping and the dead
> Are but as pictures. 'Tis the eye of childhood
> That fears a painted devil. If he do bleed,
> I'll gild the faces of the grooms withal,
> For it must seem their guilt.
>
> (II.ii.52-56)

Macbeth

Her entire effort of depersonalization lies compressed within the notorious pun: an inner condition of being ("guilt") is to be externalized into sheer theatrical appearance ("gilt"), not simply to transfer it onto others but to empty it of the substance of reality and make it (stage-)manageable. Her repeated assurance that "A little water clears us of this deed" (II.ii.66) would similarly transmute the red and real blood of Duncan not simply into gilt but into something as superficial and removable as the Elizabethan equivalent of ketchup or greasepaint: "How easy is it then!" There is bad faith here of course, in so far as her transformation never loses consciousness of its own theatricality and thus never becomes complete. She would qualify herself for murder by becoming a devil, but to her devils remain only "painted," thereby disqualifying herself for murder. Lady Macbeth's attempt to theatricalize herself into a callous instrument of darkness and thereby disburden herself of the horror of the time is doomed to break down, largely because it receives no external confirmation or reinforcement from her husband—since role-playing in drama as in culture does not go on in a vacuum—who is constitutionally unable to think of these deeds after these ways.

In contrast to her fragile and ambivalent commitment to a mode of imitation which is expedient, temporary, and only skin-deep, Macbeth's commitment is to a mode of vision in which sign and meaning coincide, role and self are indivisible, and an action is not imitated but accomplished, once and for all time. It is a way of thinking and seeing much closer to that of Macduff, who describes the scene of the murder as "the great doom's image" (II.iii.74), than to that of his wife:

> This Duncan
> Hath borne his faculties so meek, hath been
> So clear in his great office, that his virtues
> Will plead like angels, trumpet-tongued against
> The deep damnation of his taking-off;

A Painted Devil

> And pity, like a naked new-born babe
> Striding the blast, or heaven's cherubin horsed
> Upon the sightless couriers of the air,
> Shall blow the horrid deed in every eye
> That tears shall drown the wind.
>
> (I.vii.16-25)

In Macbeth's apocalyptic and allegorical projection of the deed and its consequences, Duncan becomes the Christ-like victim, and Macbeth the Judas-like traitor and Herod-like judge who will himself be judged. With its winds, weeping, pleading, and trumpet-tongued angels, the imagined scene conflates features of several typologically related cycle plays, notably those of the Crucifixion and Last Judgment. Within a mode of vision that blurs distinctions between intent and action, subject and object, illusion and reality, even to contemplate such a deed is to shake and crack the "single state of man" in which role and self were formerly united in the figure of Duncan's trusted defender. "To know my deed," he tells his wife after the murder, "'twere best not know myself" (II.ii.72), and for Macbeth the rest of the play is dedicated to assimilating himself to the role he has fully foreseen to replace his old one, to closing any gap that remains between himself and it:

> From this moment
> The very firstlings of my heart shall be
> The firstlings of my hand. And even now,
> To crown my thoughts with acts, be it thought
>   and done:
> The castle of Macduff I will surprise,
> Seize upon Fife, give to th' edge o' th' sword
> His wife, his babes. . . .
>   No boasting like a fool;
> This deed I'll do before this purpose cool.
>
> (IV.i.146-154)

A new and antithetical unity of being is born. Macbeth expounds and enacts a philosophy of language in relation to

Macbeth

action that brings him into line with every previous tyrant of the medieval and Tudor stage. Tamburlaine's insistence on the instantaneous convertibility of his words into deeds is notorious, but the same attitude underlies Cambyses' murderous demonstrations of his omnipotence, as well as the decrees of Pharaoh, Herod, and Caesar that all the children shall be slain and all the world taxed. In each case, the tyrant enacts a demonic parody of the divine power he claims, namely the power to make the word flesh. By the end of his play, Macbeth's assimilation of himself to the dictates of the tyrant's role within the older drama being mounted by Malcolm and Macduff would seem to be complete, their dramatic visions having joined into one.

Given that the Macbeths willingly take on and play out the roles of "butcher" and "fiend-like queen" assigned to them in the apocalyptic history of Scotland according to Malcolm and Macduff, how can we contend that they are anything more than the walking moral emblems that the latter say they are, or that their play is anything essentially different from its medieval models? The answer is already implicit in the nature of their role-playing. For the fact is that, despite the different attitudes they bring to their role-playing and the different outcomes of it, Macbeth and Lady Macbeth both have to strain very hard to play out their respective roles, and neither is completely successful in doing so. Lady Macbeth cannot fully become the fiend she tries to be, and Macbeth cannot fully become the strutting and fretting Herod he thinks he is. In the case of Lady Macbeth, her eventual madness is the index of the very humanity she would negate by turning herself into a pure and untrammeled role, the residue of an untransmuted humanity that had sought boldness in drink and was checked by remembered filial ties before performing the act that should have been second nature. Madness in Shakespeare's tragedies always attests to the incompleteness of an unreinforced role-playing, that technique by which the self in its naked frailty seeks refuge from the anxiety of such extreme and disruptive actions as revenge, regicide, or abdication

A Painted Devil

through the adoption of an older and simpler mode of being. In this respect, the "antic disposition" of Hamlet, the madness of Lear on the heath, and now the quiet somnambulism of Lady Macbeth are very different from the behavior of Herod, who "ragis in the pagond and in the street also"[12] when he fails to find confirmation of his absolute kingship in the prophecies, the wise men, and events themselves. For Herod does not and cannot *go* mad; he *is* mad. His "rage" is his role, and no matter how often he is traumatized, he will rebound with cartoon-like resiliency to his former outline, and rage again.

To define the truer madness that occurs in Shakespeare's tragedies, however: what is it but to be something other than role? Those who would follow Malcolm, Macduff, and the rest in equating Lady Macbeth with her fiend-like role and Macbeth with his role of butchering tyrant, and proceed to moralize or patronize them accordingly, are simply not listening:

Macduff. Turn, hellhound, turn!
Macbeth. Of all men else I have avoided thee,
   But get thee back! My soul is too much charged
   With blood of thine already.

(v.vii.3-6)

Macduff's challenge proceeds programmatically out of his own role of missionary, Christ-like avenger. Yet Macbeth's response proceeds not out of his assigned and chosen role of stage-tyrant, but out of an unsuspected reserve of sympathetic and spontaneous humanity that exists beneath it, a self still fragile and unhardened in evil even at this point, against his own and Macduff's protestations and accusations to the contrary. And Shakespeare's juxtaposition of the two reveals how inadequate and inappropriate are the moral terms deriving from the didactic drama of Satan, Pharaoh, Herod, Cambyses, even Richard III, to the drama of Macbeth.

[12] *Two Coventry Corpus Christi Plays*, p. 27.

Macbeth

Shakespeare makes it clear that Macbeth's play is in a fundamental sense *not* their play, despite the efforts of the characters within it, including Macbeth, to conform it to an orthodox tyrant play, and the many resemblances that result. Consider, for example, the nature of the prophecies and the manner in which they are accomplished. Just as Herod had questioned the Magi (and in one version his own interpreters), Macbeth questions the witches. He is shown in a highly archaic dumb-show an emblem of a "Child Crowned, with a tree in his hand" and another of a "Bloody Child," with accompanying glosses to the effect that "none of woman born / Shall harm Macbeth" and "Macbeth shall never vanquished be until / Great Birnam Wood to high Dunsinane Hill / Shall come against him" (IV.i.80-81, 92-94). Malcolm's camouflaging of his troops with the foliage of Birnam Wood identifies him with the crowned child bearing a branch, Macduff's Caesarean birth identifies him with the bloody child, and together they do indeed overcome Macbeth, with all the irony of a violated nature having her vengeance on the man who has violated her workings in himself. Yet even as these prophecies come true, they do so with an air of contrivance and artificiality quite alien to the inevitability of those of the cycle plays. On the religious stage the prophecies had had a literal transparency that those of *Macbeth* no longer possess. No interpretive effort is necessary to reconcile what was predicted (a king is to be born who will supplant Herod) and what occurred; or the literal meaning of the prophecy (Christ will supplant Herod) and its moral meaning (good will supplant evil); or the signs in which the prophecy is expressed (a star in the sky like a "sun"; a word in a sacred text) and their significance (the "son" of God, the "word made flesh").

In *Macbeth*, by contrast, a strenuous interpretive effort is necessary to reconcile the portentous emblems and pronouncements of the witches' dumb-show with their human and natural fulfillments, though we are largely unconscious of that effort when we make it. This is not simply a matter

A Painted Devil

of the trickiness traditionally associated with prophecies of demonic origin. For not only are the prophecies of *Macbeth* not transparent and univocal as the prophecies of the Herod plays had been; strictly speaking, they do not even come true. It is not Birnam Wood but Malcolm's army bearing branches from Birnam Wood that comes against Macbeth at Dunsinane. Macduff may have been "Untimely ripped" from his mother's womb, making him something of a man apart, but that hardly qualifies him as one not "of woman born," the immaculate and other-worldly avenger of a fallen Scotland. It is only when we suppress their literal meaning (and our own literalism) and take the prophecies solely at a figurative level that they can be said to "come true" at all, let alone be made to illustrate the kind of moral logic we like to read out of them. In his handling of the prophecies so as to reveal their "double sense," their disjuncture of literal and figurative meanings, Shakespeare has introduced an element of parody, of fallen repetition, into his play in relation to its medieval models.

Yet this parodic discrepancy between Christian vision and Shakespearean revision which runs through the play does not in the least prevent the Scottish resurgents from blithely conducting themselves and their counterplot as if no such gap existed and the two were one and the same, even though their own elected roles and exalted design are compromised by it. We might think, for example, that Macduff's unexplained abandonment of his own children and wife to Macbeth's tyranny, though ultimately providing him with the most natural of motives for revenge, could scarcely strengthen his claim to the exalted, impersonal role of Scotland's avenger prescribed by the play's Christian model. After all, even on the medieval stage it is the epic, superhuman Christ of the Apocalypse who harrows hell, and not the more human figure of the gospels. But for the Scottish resurgents, these deeds must not be thought of after these ways. It is precisely their capacity to sublimate their naked frailties into the service of a missionary role and a divine

Macbeth

plan that constitutes their real strength and the prerequisite for their success. Macduff's personal guilt and grief are instantly transformed, at Malcolm's prompting, into the "whetstone" of his sword in the impending divine conflict, for which "the pow'rs above / Put on their instruments" (IV.iii.238-249). As such an "instrument" of righteousness, Macduff "wants the natural touch" (IV.ii.9) in more ways than his wife imagines. His unhesitating absorption into his role is never more astonishing than when he finally presents his own nativity legend, however literally lacking it may be, as the necessary credential for defeating Macbeth, however invincible in combat he once again appears. The same absence of self-doubt or self-consciousness in his new kingly role also characterizes Malcolm (whose single act prior to the mounting of the counterplot was also one of flight), particularly in his disposition of that "Which would be planted newly with the time" (v.viii.65) after the final victory. His announced intent of rewarding his followers with promotion to the rank of earl and of punishing his foes ("The cruel ministers / Of this dead butcher and his fiend-like queen" [v.viii.68-69]) sets the seal on the new historical order of his reign as a secular imitation of divine judgment. Yet the scene is also an eerie and unsettling repetition of an earlier scene in the play. For Malcolm's language and gestures cannot help but recall those of Duncan after the victory over Cawdor and Macdonwald, a new era of freedom and love that proved only too fragile and temporary, anything but an apocalyptic triumph of good over evil. The battle toward a civilized and humane order, like all the play's battles would seem only to have been lost and won after all. The arrival of Malcolm and Macduff at Dunsinane is decidedly not the harrowing of hell or the coming of Christ, though its partisans behave as if it were.

Of course it is not really surprising that Macduff and Malcolm never come to perceive, much less feel, themselves to inhabit the gap between the heroic and archaic roles they adopt and the precarious selves that adopt them. For they

A Painted Devil

are ultimately akin to such earlier Shakespearean tragic foils as Laertes and Edgar, un-self-conscious and un-self-questioning imitators of an inherited and wholly conventional way of acting, two-dimensional characters in a three-dimensional world. It makes no difference whether we say that such foils seem cardboard or cut-to-pattern because they are supporting actors or that they are doomed to be supporting actors because they are cardboard and cut-to-pattern. For it is precisely the conventionality of Laertes' rant and Edgar's mock-madness that throws into relief the dimensionality of Hamlet's and Lear's more demanding experience. We can accept in them an unreflectiveness, even an insensitivity that is harder to accept or understand in Shakespeare's protagonists themselves. We are not unsettled when Laertes acts like Laertes, rants for revenge and leaps into his sister's grave. The cat will mew, the dog will have his day. It is much more unsettling, however, when Hamlet acts like Laertes, betrays the very depth and sensitivity that distinguishes him from Laertes, and does the same. Similarly, no one is shocked when Macduff enters with "the tyrant's cursed head" atop a pike and apocalyptically proclaims that "The time is free" (v.viii.55), nor when Malcolm lends his blessing to the deed and the sentiment. For that judicial brutality and the ritual language that surrounds it proceed directly out of the ingenuous repetition of convention that we have come to expect from these characters and violate nothing that has been shown to exist in either of them. Macbeth's brutalities, by contrast, and the self-brutalization that makes them possible are profoundly disturbing to us, not simply because they remain so disturbing to him, and not simply because they represent, as one critic puts it, "murder by thesis"[13]—for what else is Macduff's decapita-

---

[13] "It [Macbeth's atrocity against Macduff's family] is not nursed malice (they are 'unfortunate' souls), but murder for thesis, a deed in which all that makes an act recognisably human, whether moral or immoral, has been by-passed." Wilbur Sanders, *The Dramatist and the Received Idea* (Cambridge, 1968), p. 270. That the impulse behind

Macbeth

tion of Macbeth?—but because they betray precisely that fullness of humanity with which Shakespeare has endowed *him* in contrast to his foils. In his strenuous effort to become the complete tyrant, to achieve the demonic equivalent of his angelic foils' un-self-conscious conventionality, Macbeth must go out of his way to ignore the gap he senses between the pious and preordained view of things and the way things are, must do willfully what the others do quite naturally.

The question arises, then, why does Macbeth accept his destiny as a latter-day Herod, when he is not Herod? For no less remarkable than Macduff's unhesitating conviction that his birth carries the necessary credential for defeating him, is Macbeth's unresisting acceptance of it and the consequent slackening of his "better part of man." Why does Macbeth acquiesce to prophecies that require his cooperation to be fulfilled? The answer to these questions, I would suggest, lies in the mode of vision that we have already seen him bring to his experience before the murder of Duncan. He simply cannot do otherwise, not because his actions are compelled from without—the prophecies are not theologically binding like those of the cycle plays but psychologically self-fulfilling[14]—but because he has long since

---

Macbeth's "thesis" of dehumanization remains "recognizably human" and hardly as alienating in its effect as Sanders claims is confirmed by the fact that he can still call his victims "unfortunate," that he adopts it precisely for its promise of destroying his human sympathies, and that he never completely achieves its aim of self-demonization. Sanders' essay, in its responsiveness to the dramatic phenomenon of *Macbeth* and resistance to the received moral ideas that surround it, represents a genuine advance in interpretation of the play despite occasional atavisms.

[14] By changing their nature from the "goddesses of destinie" of Holinshed's *Chronicle* to Elizabethan witches, Shakespeare subtly but significantly curtails the weird sisters' power of determination. It is now Macbeth's actions that make the prophecies "come true" and not the prophecies that reveal a predetermined truth. Of course he will be conquered when Birnam Wood comes to Dunsinane, but only if

A Painted Devil

internalized his society's way of seeing and thinking. Both before and after the murder, Macbeth's is a primitive and animistic world of portents and totems, of stones that "prate" of his whereabouts, of a bell that summons to heaven or hell, of knocking that might raise the dead, of the crow turned emblem of darkness, of night that is synonymous with evil, of accusing voices and menacing visions, a world become archaic melodrama burdened with significance. This "overperception," in which distinctions between subject and object, man and nature, illusion and reality, past and present—all the potential distinctions of our modern critical and historical consciousness—are lost, is characterized in its essence by Lady Macbeth, when she reminds her husband that " 'Tis the eye of childhood / That fears a painted devil," that "these flaws and starts . . . would well become / A woman's story at a winter's fire, / Authorized by her grandam" (III.iv.63-66). Yet it is just such a childlike and superstitious vision that finally binds everyone else in the play, including Macbeth, into a society as traditional and cohesive as a tribe or a clan. It is the vocation of the ruling and priestly class of such a society to paint, fear, and punish the devils who endanger that cohesiveness and their own power, and this is exactly what the Scottish thanes do, from the suppression of Macdonwald and Cawdor to the overthrow of Macbeth. The act of mounting atop a pole Macdonwald's and Macbeth's painted images, or better still their heads, is necessary as a totemic deterrent to tyranny, a public symbol of the inviolability of the social order and a glaring reminder of the inevitability of the moral law that sustains it: the wages of ambition is, and always must be, death. Macbeth had been an integral part of this social order, as Cawdor had been, so

---

he leaves his seige-proof castle to meet it; of course he must beware Macduff, once he slaughters his family; of course Macduff alone has the power to harm Macbeth, but only when Macbeth recognizes him as one not of woman born. On the grounding of the prophecies in a purely natural "law of retributive reaction," see the excellent discussion by Sanders, pp. 253-307.

Macbeth

it is in no way surprising to see them both attempt to conform their careers to the sacred fictions they were born into and carry around within them, Cawdor by repenting like a morality protagonist and Macbeth by remaining the arch tyrant to the end. Macbeth and Macduff understand one another perfectly, across the moral gulf that separates them, for both speak the primitive language of the tribe.

This is not to suggest that Shakespeare is simply holding up to ridicule the sacred myths, symbols, and forms that so pervade *Macbeth*. It is Marlowe, not Shakespeare, who is given to expressing an adolescent contempt for religion as something invented to "keep men in awe."[15] The play is much more than an easy demystification of the ritual forms that dominate the consciousness and condition the actions of virtually all its principals, for it shows those forms to be at once quite arbitrary and fictive in themselves but wholly necessary and "real" in the social function they serve. In this respect, the play presents a stylization not only of Shakespeare's own society, where these Christian, ritual forms still prevail, but of all societies. It would be the height of ethnocentric naivete to view the "ecstatic" or "nostalgic" community depicted in *Macbeth* as any more primitive in its constitution than later, more "enlightened" societies in which heads are no longer mounted on poles.[16] The gibbet in the eighteenth century—some of whose

---

[15] Marlowe's religious views and the testimony of Thomas Kyd and Richard Baines, quoted here, are intelligently discussed by J. B. Steane, *Marlowe: A Critical Study* (Cambridge, 1964), pp. 17-26.

[16] The term "ecstatic" is aptly applied to Shakespeare's tragic societies by Northrop Frye, *Fools of Time* (Toronto, 1967), p. 29, and "nostalgic" by Alvin Kernan, "*The Henriad*: Shakespeare's Major History Plays," *The Yale Review*, LIX (1969), 1, 3-32, to the older, passing world of the second tetralogy. The concept is further elaborated by Maynard Mack, Jr., *Killing the King* (New Haven, 1972). It is worth noting that the object Macduff carries in the closing scene of D'Avenant's revision of the play (1674) is not Macbeth's "head" but his "sword." The substitution, part of a larger effort to render Shakespeare seemly by rendering him bloodless, works to obscure the primitive essence of the Scottish society of Shakespeare's play and the underlying similarity between Macduff and Macbeth as creatures of it.

A Painted Devil

Shakespearean criticism does indeed condescend to his Elizabethan "barbarism,"—or the electric chair in the twentieth are designed to serve the same necessary function of deterring deviance within the community and to preserve the same necessary fiction that crime must inevitably be followed, as the night the day, by punishment. Moreover, the play depicts the impulse constitutive of every society to make its particular social forms and institutions, which are always arbitrary in so far as they are man-made, seem as necessary as natural forms and processes themselves, indeed a logical extension of them:

> I have begun to plant thee and will labor
> To make thee full of growing.
> (I.iv.28-29)

> What's more to do,
> Which would be planted newly with the time—
> As calling home our exiled friends abroad. . . .
> (v.viii.64-66)

> My way of life
> Is fall'n into the sear, the yellow leaf. . . .
> (v.iii.22-26)

Within a world that sees itself through the ritual forms of the medieval drama, in which the book of human history and the book of nature are one volume of God's making, it is almost a reflex of all its members to describe the social and historical process of meting out rewards and punishments, for all its demonstrated fallibility, in an imagery of unfailing natural process. But to dismiss this impulse as a version of nostalgic fiction or pathetic fallacy is to misunderstand the play. For like Macbeth's, Duncan's, Lennox's, and the others' investment of the natural world with human attributes, these efforts to endow the human and historical world with a serene inevitability that properly belongs only to non-human nature is more than fiction and

Macbeth

less than truth, another aspect of the persistent recreation of the sacred, the remystification of the merely secular, that defines the world of the play in its essential doubleness.

It is this radical equivocation of *Macbeth* in relation to its medieval models, the double sense in which it at once recreates those models through the communal effort of its characters and reveals them to be a means of social and institutional legitimation, that makes the play so susceptible to pious mystification or ironic demystification. Of these possibilities for misinterpretation, the pious reading has of course prevailed. The play is generally regarded as a humanization and vivification, through the flesh and blood of Shakespeare's mature language and dramaturgy, of the bare skeleton of its stagy and didactic antecedents. In this view, their homiletic intent though it may be softened is not fundamentally questioned or altered in the process of benign and respectful transformation. The "good" characters are granted just enough of a depth they do not possess, and the "evil" characters are denied just enough of the depth they do possess, to flatten the play into a consistent domestication of a wholly traditional moral design. But surely it must be otherwise, for in what does Shakespeare's humanization of his sources consist but the putting into question of their conventional roles and forms? To the extent that the figures who carry around with them that older moral design as a sacred and un-self-conscious trust are made to appear conventional, predictable, and bidimensional by contrast with the figures with whom they share the stage and who are restless in their roles, however strenuously they attempt to conform to them, that older moral design can no longer be authoritative. Critics have always been responsive to the interiority of Macbeth's struggle, but they have been reluctant to recognize that it is achieved precisely at the expense of his status as a moral emblem or example. Yet he becomes something much more interesting to us than any moral emblem in the process, and not because, as the critical commonplace would have it, evil is intrinsically more interesting than good. Macbeth is more interesting than his prototypes and foils, not because they are good and he becomes evil—for Herod is hardly "good"—nor even because they "are" and he "becomes"—for his change is in many ways regressive—but because he cannot take his nature for granted. He cannot quite rest content in an action in which his role and his nature are determined in advance, but must continuously re-invent himself in the process of acting them out. It is in this that Macbeth's "modernity" consists and that his case bears directly on our own, at least to the extent that we are as fully human as he is. In this respect too, he becomes a very different kind of dramatic model, a type of modernity whose compelling interest for the playwrights who follow Shakespeare will cause him to be imitated again and again.

The simplifications that have become doctrine in the tradition of interpretation of *Macbeth* are the result not only of a failure to establish the play's relation to its models in its full ambivalence, but of a failure to identify the play's primary models in the first place. Just as *Hamlet* has less to do with Senecan revenge drama than with native morality tradition, so *Macbeth* has less to do with the morality play than with the tyrant plays of the Biblical cycles. Its nearest contemporary analogue is not Marlowe's *Faustus*, with which it is often compared as a parallel study in the psychology of damnation,[17] but *Tamburlaine* or even *Edward*

[17] See, for example, Helen Gardner, "Milton's Satan and the Theme of Damnation in Elizabethan Tragedy," *Essays and Studies*, 1 (1948), 42-61. The fundamental inappropriateness of morality models to *Macbeth* is also apparent from D'Avenant's version, where Macbeth is reduced to a personification of Tyranny and Ambition (at his death, the stage direction reads "Ambition dies"), and the sharpest possible moral contrast, summed up in Macduff's closing couplet, is aimed at: "His Vice shall make your Virtue shine more Bright, / As a Fair Day succeeds a Stormy Night." The moralization of the play is carried a stage further toward absurdity in Garrick's additions to J. P. Kemble's

Macbeth

II, those early Elizabethan history plays which, like *Macbeth*, are modeled on the medieval tyrant plays that are the authentic prototypes of Elizabethan historical tragedy. The morality play is a misleading model in the interpretation of *Macbeth* in so far as it presents a world already more cerebral and voluntaristic than the cultic and animistic world of the cycles. It emphasizes, that is, freedom of moral choice within a mental setting, as opposed to the communal and typological destiny unfolded in the cycles. This misplaced emphasis on moral choice within *Macbeth*, where it receives little of the extended deliberation accorded to it in *Hamlet*, may well arise from the forced imposition of morality conventions upon the play and may well underlie all the misguided adulation of the bland and reticent Banquo and the equally misguided pity for Macbeth. For Macbeth's choices and actions, as I have tried to show, are not free in the way the morality protagonist's are, but are largely determined by his own and his society's expectations soon after the play begins. The universe of *Macbeth* is not ultimately and comically free, as it is even in those variations of the morality (like *Faustus*) where the protagonist persists in choosing wrongly and thus qualifies as an object of tragic pity, but is conditioned by forces largely outside his control. Of course those forces are no longer the benign and providential ones embodied in the figures of God and his angels who descend from above upon the human com-

---

acting copy (1795), in which Macbeth becomes a pale and frightened Faustus before his death:

> Ambition's vain delusive dreams are fled,
> And now I wake to darkness, guilt and horror;
> I cannot bear it! let me shake it off—
> It will not be; my soul is clog'd with blood—
> I cannot rise! I dare not ask for mercy—
> It is too late, hell drags me down; I sink,
> I sink,—my soul is lost for ever!—Oh!—Oh!—*Dies*.

Reprinted by H. H. Furness, ed., Variorum *Macbeth* (Philadelphia, 1873), pp. 355, 295.

A Painted Devil

munity below. Rather, they are disruptive forces that periodically and inexplicably bubble up, as it were, from within human nature and society, as the witches who incarnate and herald them seem to do from within the earth itself. Unlike the morality protagonist, who is confronted at all points with a clear choice between moral meanings already established by generations of sophisticated theological apologetics, Macbeth, and the protagonist of Elizabethan historical tragedy generally, must struggle with meaning as it ambiguously unfolds in the world. It is only by confusing these two dramatic modes that such reassuring commonplaces as "the Elizabethan world picture" or "the great chain of being" could misleadingly have been applied as a norm in the interpretation of Shakespeare's histories and tragedies in the first place, as if the "natural condition" they present were order and the life of man could be analogized to the life of nonhuman nature. In our own struggle with the meaning of *Macbeth*, the proper identification of those models actually implicit within the play thus proves crucial and affirms once again the interdependence of literary history and interpretation.

CHAPTER 5

"Jacobean Decadence": Tourneur, Middleton, Webster, Ford

>   I would have our plot be ingenious,
>   And have it hereafter recorded for example
>   Rather than borrow example.
>   —*The White Devil*, v.i.74-76

THE NOTION that literary history evolves through distinct phases of development like the natural history of an organism or a species is at least as ancient as Aristotle. Aristotle, in fact, includes a brief history of Attic tragedy in the *Poetics*, tracing its major technical mutations from its origins in the choric song and dance of the dithyramb, through Aeschylus' introduction of a second actor, to Sophocles' addition of a third actor and scene painting. With Sophocles, tragedy reached its "height" or "full magnitude" (*megethos*). "Tragedy advanced by slow degrees," he concludes; "each new element that showed itself was in turn developed. Having passed through many changes, it found its nature (*physin*), and there it stopped" (IV.12).[1] The passage, though concerned only with the outward form of Greek tragedy, can be seen as the starting-point for most subsequent histories of that drama. The multiplication of technical resources described by Aristotle suggests a development from religious ritual toward stage naturalism; we

[1] Quotations in my text are from *Aristotle's Poetics*, trans. by Leon Golden, with commentary by O. B. Hardison, Jr. (Englewood Cliffs, 1968).

"Jacobean Decadence"

move from the ritualistic drama of Aeschylus through the heroic realism of Sophocles to the ironic or debased realism of Euripides. This stylistic development is often said to be conditioned by, or reflective of, the course of Athenian social and political history. The growth of high tragedy in Aeschylus and Sophocles coincides with the consolidation of Athenian power following the repulse of Persia, and the Euripidean decline with the disintegration of Athens in the Peloponnesian War. In recent years especially, Euripides has been defended against older charges of decadence or eccentricity, but because these revaluations perpetuate the older view of Euripides as a "poet of his time," they invariably take on the sound of special pleading and apologetics. The poet of a decadent time cannot help, in such a literary-historical view, but reflect the decadence of his time:[2] if Sophocles is the model of tragic maturity and Euripides both comes after and departs from Sophoclean practice, then Euripides must represent a falling-off into decline or decay.

It should be pointed out, however, that neither the idea of a Euripidean decline nor that of literary history as reflecting or refracting cultural history exists in Aristotle. The opening phrase of the *Poetics*, "On the art of poetry

[2] The following passage illustrates most of the circularities and banalities that characterize the prevailing literary historicism: "It was life, not Euripides, which had abandoned the traditional forms and the traditional heroism. What Euripides reported, with great clarity and honesty, was the widening gulf between reality and tradition; between the operative and the professed values of his culture; between fact and myth; between *nomos* and *physis*; between life and art. That gulf was the greatest and most evident reality of the last half of the fifth century, *the* dramatic subject par excellence, and it is my belief that the theater of Euripides . . . is a radical and revolutionary attempt to record, analyze, and assess that reality in relation to the new view of human nature which crisis revealed." William Arrowsmith, "A Greek Theater of Ideas," in *Ideas in the Drama*, ed. John Gassner (New York, 1964). Was there ever a time or a culture in which these "gulfs" were *not* "widening" or at least "wide"? And was there ever an authentic writer *not* engaged in "a radical and revolutionary attempt to record, analyze, and assess that reality"?

in itself" (*Peri poietikes autes*), suggests that poetry in general and tragedy in particular are to be considered as autonomous activities quite apart from the historical or biographical context within which they are produced. Even the famous definition of poetry as "the imitation of an action" (*mimesis praxeos*) by no means refers unequivocally to an empirical action to be paraphrased by "life" or "reality" or "experience" or "history"; more probably it refers to the abstract and idealized action later designated by the more formal and literary word "plot" (*mythos*). It is only by literalizing the biological metaphor implicit in "Having passed through many changes, it [tragedy] found its nature" that the idea of a Euripidean decline can be read out of Aristotle at all, but Aristotle offers no warrant for such a reading, in fact, denies all implications of decay by adding, "*and there it stopped.*"

The apparent shift from a biological to a teleological vocabulary in this remarkable passage is not really a shift at all, since for the pre-Darwinian Aristotle, biology is teleology. All nature is consistently described as moving toward the perfect realization of its various kinds, from which no decline is necessary, and literary kinds are no exception. Because this perfect realization of tragic form is achieved earlier, more often, and more consistently by Sophocles than by Euripides, Aristotle does express some ambivalence toward the latter: "faulty though he [Euripides] may be in the general management of his subject" (XIII.6); "it [the Chorus] should be an integral part of the whole, and share in the action, in the manner not of Euripides but of Sophocles" (XVIII.7); "he [quoting Sophocles with approval] drew men as they ought to be: Euripides, as they are" (XXV.6). Throughout the *Poetics*, Euripides represents not so much a decadent offspring of Sophoclean maturity as a departure from a tragic norm more or less Sophoclean, but one which could still be followed at any chronological point. A revaluation of Euripides' work that wished to remain consistent with an Aristotelian poetics would avoid

"Jacobean Decadence"

historical rationalizations and show that Euripides' deviations from Sophoclean practice are part of a consistent strategy of reaction against Sophocles that puts into question Sophocles' claim to be the only tragic norm. Aristotle fairly invites such a project when he calls Euripides, somewhat inconsistently, "the most tragic of the poets." (XIII.9).

Though my subject in this essay is not Greek tragedy but Elizabethan tragedy, the case of Euripides and his relation to his predecessors is paradigmatic. For we encounter a similar situation in the historiography of Elizabethan drama, where the notion of a Jacobean "decadence" following the mature tragic achievements of Marlowe and especially Shakespeare is still deeply ingrained. Here Marlowe corresponds to Aeschylus, taking over the ritual forms of the medieval stage, freeing their conventions of stiffness and their language of doggerel, and creating almost singlehandedly the kind of drama we know as Elizabethan. Shakespeare then becomes the English Sophocles, developing, refining, and consolidating the daring innovations of Marlowe into a mature and universal vision, a fullness of tragic form from which only decline would seem to be possible. Among the major Jacobean playwrights—Tourneur-Middleton,[3] Webster, and Ford—it is Webster who is our Euripides, though they all share in some degree this dubious destiny of literary history. For Webster is the primary focus of charges leveled at some time against them all, charges of lurid sensationalism, morbid interest in death and decay, preoccupation with abnormal psychology, an absence of moral norms—symptoms of Jacobean decadence, all.

This is not to suggest that these and other Jacobean playwrights are universally condemned. On the contrary, from the time of Lamb onward the Elizabethan and Jacobean drama has, if anything, been the object of an often uncrit-

---

[3] I employ this composite term not to suggest collaboration but to avoid the continuing debate over the authorship of Tourneur's plays. My concern in this chapter, as elsewhere, is not with the claims of dead playwrights but with the meaning of living plays.

ical and sentimental adulation. This was our golden age; these playwrights, after all, breathed the same air, trod the same streets, as Shakespeare did. Yet for all the critical appreciation, there is an audible undertone of disapprobation; they are just not Shakespearean enough. Although the good that they did was Shakespearean, the bad was their own, or perhaps, their time's. For here too a historicist "explanation" has been offered. The fault, dear reader, may not be in the playwrights themselves, but in the times they reflect or refract. After all, was not Shakespeare the beneficiary of a rare conjunction of favoring circumstances: an emerging nation; a new political stability; an audience unified by common values and beliefs; an inherently poetic, because as yet unstandardized, language; a responsiveness to poetic subtlety born of an oral culture; and so on? Look to the changing times to explain the Jacobeans: uncertainty over the impending succession; dissatisfaction with James's rule; anxiety over the challenge to established beliefs posed by the "new philosophy" of Copernican science; new political threats from Italy and Spain. That this once highly fashionable thesis has been largely discredited *on its own terms* does not prevent it from reappearing in more subtle guises in the criticism of Jacobean drama.[4] But even among those critics who value Webster and his contemporaries most highly, they are often valued *for their Shakespearean qualities*. Beneath the shifting surfaces of Webster's dramaturgy, we are told, lies a Shakespearean firmness of control; his moral indeterminacy resolves into a clear and traditional moral vision; his relativism rivals Shakespeare's own characteristic balance and ambiguity; he even shows a Shakespearean sympathy for the meanest of his creatures. Much of the

[4] See "The Elizabethan and the Jacobean Shakespeare" in R. W. Chambers, *Man's Unconquerable Mind* (London, 1939), pp. 250-276. This essay, as fully traditional and historicist as the thesis it refutes, clearly demonstrates that contemporary pronouncements of "gloom" can be counterbalanced or even outweighed by pronouncements of "optimism."

"Jacobean Decadence"

best criticism of Webster takes this approach of praising him in terms of another playwright's virtues, as when T. S. Eliot, for example, sees Webster, along with Tourneur, as being closest to Shakespeare in inspiration.[5]

As long as Webster and his contemporaries are regarded as epiphenomena in the evolutionary historicism that produced Shakespeare, a view that necessarily limits their claim to voluntarism and self-consciousness as dramatists in their own right, their distinctive achievement cannot fully or clearly emerge. The terms of that achievement having been prejudiced by their assumed tutelage as Shakespeare's offspring or disciples, all sympathetic perceptions of their work are capable at any point of being turned back into the older, less sympathetic ones, the artistic priority of Shakespeare as the implicit or explicit standard of comparison never having been put into question. After surveying modern criticism of Webster and acknowledging its many local insights, G. K. Hunter concludes that "something is still lacking." "This might be described," he continues, "as a simplification of the truths already known. We ought to be able to formulate a 'general law' which will describe all the instances in their basic terms. When this is written it may then be possible to return to the question of Webster's relation to Shakespeare and his other contemporaries without seeing him too simply as either decadent or aberrant."[6] These two projects may, in fact, turn out to be one. The "general law" of Websterian effects that Hunter seeks may arise out of the effort to establish the nature of the Jacobeans' relation to Shakespeare. In any event, a coherent theory of the Jacobeans' relation to Shakespeare remains a desideratum in the interpretation of the work of each of them.

In the attempt to reconstruct that relation in a way that is neither prejudicial nor oversimplifying, we will reach

---

[5] *Selected Essays* (New York, 1932), p. 161.

[6] *John Webster: A Critical Anthology*, edd. G. K. and S. K. Hunter (Baltimore, 1969), p. 110.

further by focusing on one definitive feature of Elizabethan dramaturgy, from which other matters can follow, and by beginning with a non-Shakespearean, but not wholly un-Shakespearean, play that exemplifies it. Thomas Heywood's *A Woman Killed with Kindness* (1603) will serve as an apposite point of departure. The play belongs to the popular Elizabethan genre of domestic tragedy—it is something of a not too poor man's *Othello*—and exemplifies the characteristic Elizabethan practice of multiple plotting. Much critical attention has been devoted of late to the subject of Elizabethan subplots, and they are now generally acknowledged, after decades of disrepute, as a principal means of enhancing the social comprehensiveness, thematic complexity, and even the dramatic unity of the plays in which they appear.[7] In the case of *A Woman Killed with Kindness*, a play frequently praised in the literary histories for the bourgeois realism of its main action, few critics have actually gone so far as to defend its highly stylized and aristocratic subplot. T. S. Eliot, for example, describes the subplot as "too grotesque even to horrify us; but it is too obviously there merely because an underplot is required to fill out the play for us to feel anything but boredom when it recurs."[8] The most that has been said for it is that its aristocratic action of honorable revenge is subordinated to its middle-class main action of prudent restraint, which is thereby endorsed by Heywood and the play, and that this inversion of dramatic and social hierarchy is an innovation.[9] That Heywood is concerned, even apologetic, about the humble realism of his play is evident in the Prologue, where "Our Poet's dull and earthy Muse"

[7] See Richard Levin, *The Multiple Plot in English Renaissance Drama* (Chicago, 1971), and Harry Levin, "The Shakespearean Overplot," *Renaissance Drama 8* (1965), 63-71. On the related phenomenon of the play-within-a-play, see Robert J. Nelson, *The Play Within a Play* (New Haven, 1958), and Arthur Brown, "The Play Within a Play: an Elizabethan Dramatic Device," *Essays and Studies* (1960), 36-48.

[8] *Selected Essays*, p. 154.

[9] See Richard Levin, *The Multiple Plot*, pp. 93-96.

and "a barren subject, a bare scene"[10] are contrasted with more traditionally exalted subject-matter and more sumptuous productions. In this regard, the subplot may indeed play a necessary role in the achievement of the play's celebrated bourgeois realism, for the realism of any work, its fundamental and essential mimetic claim on us, is never simply a function of lowly subject-matter or elaborate productions. Realism is always a relative matter. Like Prince Hal's reformation, it works by foils and "Shall show more goodly and attract more eyes / Than that which hath no foil to set it off." Realism, that is, only arises from the destruction of prior convention.

Heywood is well aware of this, and he includes the subplot in *A Woman Killed with Kindness* not primarily because it is aristocratic but because it is archaic. The convention-ridden, morality-derived, markedly unrealistic subplot serves as a necessary foil to show off the more "modern" realism of the main action. For the subplot, which presents the fall and redemption of Sir Charles Mountford and his sister Susan at the hands of Sir Francis Acton, is constructed throughout on morality principles. Its settings are distinctly emblematic: the initial hawking scene, in which the predatory instincts of their hawks are suddenly transferred to the aristocrats themselves; the field before Mountford's last remaining cottage where he has been reduced to tilling the soil and uttering speeches on the theme of "All things on earth thus change"; the "dungeon in York Castle," where Sir Charles enters "in prison, with irons, his feet bare, his garments all ragged and torn" after the causeless and boundless hatred of Acton and his band of usurious Vices has taken all from him. Motivation is similarly allegorical and morality-derived. Although their aristocratic honor and high spirits are sometimes invoked by Acton and Mountford to justify their actions, they move in a world of

[10] Quotations from Heywood are from *A Woman Killed with Kindness*, ed. R. W. Van Fossen (The Revels Plays, Cambridge, Mass., 1961).

detached and impersonal motives. "Forgive me God!" says Mountford after precipitately murdering two of Acton's men in the hawking scene and just as precipitately repenting, " 'Twas in the heat of blood, / And anger quite removes me from myself. / It was not I, but rage, did this vile murther." (iii.51-53). "Rage" could be capitalized. The motivation behind his acts of murder and repentance has little basis in social or psychological circumstance; it preexists social and psychological circumstance, a dramatic given instantly understandable to any Elizabethan audience. Of course Acton too is subject to the morality-derived logic of the plot, and we should not be surprised when his gratuitous hate for the Mountfords melts into love at the sight of Susan's face, nor even by the double act of forgiveness by which Mountford delivers up his sister to Acton's will and Acton, now "Reformed in all things" (v.9) as Mountford was earlier, elects to marry rather than deflower her. An ultimately benevolent moral universe has, in true morality fashion, been vindicated, as all hatred is redressed and all loss repaired.

In turning to the main action we enter a dramatic universe of another sort. All its elements have been fundamentally altered in relation to the foil of the subplot, not merely as a result of the social descent hinted at by Heywood and pointed out by the literary histories (more evidence of the rise of the ever-rising middle class), but in the sense of a thoroughgoing stylistic modification. Instead of shifting among emblematic scenes and tableaux, the setting of the main action is largely confined to the "real estate" of Frankford's home, bustling with the mundane activities of meals and amusement. Indeed, Frankford's house is literally "there" throughout, providing a stable contrast to the moral emblems of Acton's and Mountford's genealogical "houses." Nor do the characters of the main action behave in a manner so clearly dictated by the conventions of morality drama. Whereas the actions of betrayal, revenge, and forgiveness that make up the subplot are all under-

"Jacobean Decadence"

motivated, those of the main plot are carefully premeditated, subject to second thoughts, modified by others' opinions and external circumstances. Wendoll sorts out his motives, reproaches and remonstrates with himself, unlike Mountford, before attempting his fatal seduction; so does Anne, both before and after succumbing to him. No one behaves in the compulsive, un-self-conscious fashion of moral allegory within the main action—not even Frankford himself at the moment he discovers his friend and wife together in bed, though the temptation to do so is always close at hand:

> O me unhappy! I have found them lying
> Close in each other's arms, and fast asleep.
> But that I would not damn two precious souls,
> Bought with my Savior's blood, and send them laden
> With all their scarlet sins upon their backs
> Unto a fearful judgment, their two lives
> Had met upon my rapier.
>
> (xiii.44-50)

It is precisely this reluctance of Frankford to enter into the conventional role of just revenger of his honor, even though it is socially sanctioned and even though he repeatedly entertains it in his thoughts, that constitutes the play's most crucial departure from the dramatic mode of its subplot. That role, after all, was the pretext for Acton's prolonged persecution of Mountford, and Nick, obedient to instinct rather than a histrionic program (which is why the servant's level of action cannot develop into a full-scale plot), repeatedly urges the same course. Both, in fact, state that "and the case were mine" (xiii.36), "had it been my case" (xvii.20) nothing less would suffice than bloody revenge on wife and lover both. Frankford implicitly indicts such a morality-revenge action by deciding that " 'Twill be revenge enough" to leave them to the punishment of their own inner torment, underscoring his point by the added "kindness" of restoring all their earthly goods to them before banishing them from his house. His program works only because Wendoll and Anne do have an inner life, unlike Mountford, Susan, and Acton, for it to work on. Even Acton, who would have acted differently, *does* act differently, congratulates Frankford for his revenge of kindness on his sister, against his own previously proclaimed and enacted principles:

> Brother, had you with threats and usage bad
> Punish'd her sin, the grief of her offence
> Had not with such true sorrow touch'd her heart.
> (xvii.133-135)

Frankford, it would seem, has successfully repudiated the moralistic histrionics of revenge that govern the subplot for a new and more enlightened dramatic and ethical project. And Heywood would seem to have left behind the stylized simplifications of the morality-revenge tradition and created in their place a new kind of drama, more realistically responsive to the personal and ethical complexities of existence.

But before we join in the chorus of approval that closes the play and uphold the judgment of the literary histories, we should reconsider whether all the praise of Frankford is really justified and whether we are praising Heywood for the right reason. It could be argued that Frankford, in answering his wife's adultery with such a show of overwhelming, relentless, and finally killing kindness, is ultimately no less self-righteous and murderous than the more forthright revengers he is supposed to have transcended. His bizarre revenge of "kindness" remains a revenge and to that extent cannot really be kind at all. He kills his wife just as surely as if he had strangled her in her bed, dehumanizing her into a moral emblem in the process. In this respect, the ending of Heywood's play is not essentially different from that of the older and more overtly morality-derived *A Warning for Fair Women* (1599), with its alternately allegorical and naturalistic treatment of middle-class adultery

"Jacobean Decadence"

and uxoricide, or of *Arden of Feversham* (1591), where the wife Alice also repents of her sins and makes herself into a warning for fair wives before going to the gallows. Anne's guilt and self-loathing may lend some psychological credibility to the melodramatic convention of dying of grief and may help account for her readiness to accept so wholeheartedly the role of penitent sinner in which Frankford casts her, but it cannot extenuate the moralistic rigor with which he plays on that guilt. Pardons too can kill. Significantly, it is only Acton and his sister Anne who endorse Frankford's dramatic project without reservation. Nick distances himself from Frankford's wish—does it express compassion or his own sense of guilt?—to join her in such an exemplary death with the whimsical reminder that the sum of Frankford's moral calculation is the brute fact of death: "I'll sigh and sob, but, by my faith, not die" (xvii.103). Nor is Frankford's action so successful as it might at first appear, even in its professed aim of inducing contrition and salvation. Wendoll, the other object of his kindness, after dooming himself to exile "like a Cain," is able by the end of this parting speech to "divine (however now dejected), / My worth and parts being by some great man praised, / At my return I may in court be raised" (xvi.143-145). The morality role of "devil" and "villain" that Nick, Acton, and Anne project onto Wendoll seems finally to correspond more closely to his Vice-like resiliency than the fallible but redeemable human nature presupposed by Frankford. The morality tradition, with its simplicities and rigidities, does not die so easily as Frankford would like to think, but is reborn in the very place where it was thought to have been put gently to death, in the main action itself.

The play, then, does not so much supersede the morality tradition and replace it with a new bourgeois realism as subsume it, making it the starting-point for a mimetic revisionism that never really leaves it behind. The morality tradition may serve as a foil to set off the greater realism of a parallel action, but it also serves as an apparently inescapable touchstone of judgment on that action. For the morality, in its original form, is an ideal and purely allegorical action of which the ultimate author is God, who alone has the authority to make a play in which revenge and romance are one, and justice and peace, truth and mercy meet and kiss, as they literally do in several early examples of the form. All human attempts to imitate this divine action—whether they illustrate the middle-class virtues of prudence and restraint, as Frankford's does, or the more aristocratic ethic that "death to such deeds of shame is the due need," as Acton's, to the extent that it is a human action, does—must fall short of this divine ideal, appear wanting and inauthentic, and permit various and conflicting interpretation. To the extent, however, that such overreaching human actions and the play which shows them to be so remain deeply and continuously in touch with the divine action they naturalize and hence parody, they are necessarily morally focused, and interpretation is oriented in advance toward certain recurring ethical issues. It is therefore not surprising that no one, to my knowledge, has ever charged Heywood or his fellow Elizabethan playwrights, not even Marlowe and certainly not Shakespeare, with moral disorientation or decadence—as distinct from moral ambiguity—as critics have repeatedly charged the Jacobeans.

For the principle of parodistic structure we have seen at work in *A Woman Killed with Kindness*, by which more and less archaic actions are layered or juxtaposed within the play, precludes such a charge whenever the more archaic action is palpably morality-related, as it usually is in the popular Elizabethan drama. The effect is always the simultaneous one of mimetic naturalization and ethical problematization, but never one of moral disorientation. We encounter this structure virtually everywhere in Elizabethan drama. It is already present in the multiple plotting of *The Spanish Tragedy* (1587?), where the semi-allegorical vision of judgment that opens and frames the play and the neat

"Jacobean Decadence"

little interlude on royal justice that might be called "The Portuguese Tragicomedy" serve as dramatic foils to set off the more "naturalistic" modality of Hieronimo's efforts at revenge. These older models of legitimate retributive justice, serving as esthetic foils to Hieronimo's judicial playmaking, are also ethical reminders of an order of justice to which his all too human plotting fails to measure up. In the transcendental tragedy that frames the play, the outcome of perfect retribution is so assured and inevitable that its presiding impresario, Revenge, actually falls asleep over it. When awakened by the apprehensive Ghost of Andrea, Revenge calmly reassures him that all proceeds apace and nothing can miscarry. Similarly, in "The Portuguese Tragicomedy," just when the villainous and allegorically named Villuppo seems to have succeeded in his libelous and murderous plot against the loyal Alexandro, the truth is providentially revealed and the villain winds up, through the Viceroy's delayed but ultimately unerring sentence, on the block prepared for his victim. Both of these official or authorized myths of justice contrast sharply with Hieronimo's more fallible and frustrated efforts to imitate their structure. The bloody improvisation of revenge with which he closes the play is thus a garbled version, a veritable Babel, of these official codes in more than its linguistic medium. The guilty and innocent are indiscriminately struck down, and its presiding justice-figure Hieronimo is also a victim, forfeiting first his tongue and then his life to prevent a demeaning and disintegrative interpretation. (God's justice is of course above interpretation.) The Duke of Castile, who apparently has no knowledge of or complicity in any of his son's crimes, is murdered by Hieronimo nonetheless, presumably because he is a father, and in the parodistic logic of Hieronimo's retributive scheme, all fathers must suffer and die as he does. It remains for Revenge to pick up the pieces of Hieronimo's botchery and work its victims into the restored perfection of the "endless tragedy" that follows and transcends the play.

We encounter essentially the same principle of structure at work in Marlowe's plays, though with a difference that

Tourneur, Middleton, Webster, Ford

sometimes makes it more difficult to recognize. The difference is that Marlowe does not usually locate the archaic and authoritative foils to his main actions in parallel subplots or internal plays but implies their normative presence within the main actions themselves. This is perfectly apparent in *Doctor Faustus*, where the wholesale appropriation of morality conventions within the main action makes its morality orientation quite clear. Marlowe even introduces as a foil to Faustus' persistence in error the allegorical figure of a repentant Old Man, whose presence points the contrast between the traditional ending of the form and Faustus' own radical perversity in resisting that ending. In Marlowe's other plays, however, these archaic presences are less conspicuous to modern eyes unused to seeing them, and as a result have made these plays more resistant to interpretation. *Edward II*, for example, is a "history play" by virtue of its subject-matter, but structurally it is a "youth-morality," upon which Marlowe has worked certain changes. For the traditional figures of virtue and mature wisdom who flank the youthful figure of Edward on the one side, Marlowe substitutes the disloyal Isabel and the self-interested Mortimers. At the same time, the traditional figures of folly and temptation who flank him on the other, first Gaveston and later Spencer, prove disturbingly loyal and loving even to death. The personal and political, romantic and conservative, sides of this "moral history" are no longer mutually supportive. Marlowe's work, indeed each of his plays, demands a chapter of its own in any comprehensive history of Elizabethan drama; for our present purpose, suffice it to say that even in Marlowe, for all the subtle strength with which his plays subvert their medieval models, they still retain the older moral bearings as an interpretive frame of reference while gaining a new mimetic depth and human dimensionality.

In moving from Elizabethan and Shakespearean to Jacobean tragedy, the question remains why the dramatic universe of the latter strikes us as so different from the former, and whether this felt sense of difference, this apparent loss

"Jacobean Decadence"

of traditional moral and esthetic bearings, can be explained in terms of the principle of parodic structure we have been tracing. These questions are all the more perplexing in view of the fact that there are no major changes in the cultural situation of the popular dramatic poet, older theories of Jacobean "gloom" or "decadence" to the contrary, to account for this apparent discontinuity. The Jacobean playwrights employ the same imaginative models and share, on the whole, the audience of their Elizabethan precursors. Webster actually stresses his own continuity with Heywood, Dekker, and Shakespeare, among others of a less popular taste, in his preface to *The White Devil*, explicitly "wishing what I write may be read by their light."[11] Indeed, within the tragedies of Webster, Tourneur-Middleton, and even Ford, the older morality substructure, as we shall see directly, does not disappear but remains as visible as ever. Why then should we experience an effect of moral disorientation in their work different in kind from anything so far encountered in that of Shakespeare and the Elizabethans?

The problem can be more clearly formulated if we turn to one of the earliest of those Jacobean tragedies that have attracted the label of "decadent," Cyril Tourneur's *The Revenger's Tragedy* (1605-06). Although its imaginative power has always been acknowledged, the play was regularly seen in the earlier part of this century as an expression, in Eliot's words, of its author's "cynicism, loathing, and disgust of humanity."[12] More recently it has come to be regarded, largely as a result of an influential essay by L. G. Salingar, as a coherent reflection of a Jacobean society in transition from an older system of values based on gentility to a system of values oriented toward a new commercial opportunism.[13] Vindice's rhetoric of disgust and the corrupt court on which it is focused are to be seen not as an expression of Tour-

[11] *The White Devil*, ed. John Russell Brown (The Revels Plays, London, 1960), p. 4.

[12] *Selected Essays* (New York, 1932), p. 166.

[13] "*The Revenger's Tragedy* and the Morality Tradition," *Scrutiny*, VI (March, 1938), 402-422.

neur's personality but as a representation of contemporary social ills, a representation unified and mediated by a satiric tradition of morality drama deliberately adopted by Tourneur and familiar to his audience. The paradox latent in the older view that work of such acknowledged power could be the product of a decadent imagination might thus seem to have been resolved by this shift of critical focus from the individual talent to his tradition.

In viewing the play, however, no longer as the expression of a morbid personal vision but as a reflection of a changing Jacobean world in the glass provided by morality tradition, the decadence formerly associated with the play has merely been relocated from its author's alleged personality to the society he is allegedly holding the mirror up to. A new paradox has now replaced the old. If Tourneur is writing out of a coherent satiric tradition to reflect the debasement and commercialization of Jacobean life, why does he do so in terms of a fantastic, farcical, and Italiante world, the very stylization of which must give us pause before identifying it, with Salingar, as an imitation of an historical England? It was just such a problem of blurred satiric focus, after all, that led Ben Jonson to shift the scene of his comedies from Italy to England, thereby insuring that their moral and satiric point would not be missed. Moreover, the very fact that Tourneur could have been seen so readily and consistently as a decadent playwright in the first place, his play's conspicuous morality framework notwithstanding, stands in contrast to the reception of Kyd or Shakespeare, who also work within a morality tradition. We have already seen how the retention of a traditional frame of moral reference within their work is *precisely what prevents* their plays from falling under the charge of moral disorientation or disintegration. Yet the same technique of including a morality substructure within his work has failed, for all its conspicuousness, to prevent such a charge in the case of Tourneur. Either we are not, in fact, dealing with quite the same technique at all in *The Revenger's Tragedy* as we have been in the plays of Kyd or Shakespeare, or there is

"Jacobean Decadence"

something else, as yet unidentified, at work in Tourneur's play that might enable so traditional and morality-related a work to be so morally disorienting.

In the effort to identify this crucial difference between the dramatic practices of Tourneur and Shakespeare, let us briefly reconsider *The Revenger's Tragedy* in relation to the tradition of morality drama that provides both playwrights with their primary dramatic models:[14]

> Duke; royal lecher; go, grey-hair'd adultery;
> And thou his son, as impious steep'd as he;
> And thou his bastard, true-begot in evil;
> And thou his duchess, that will do with devil.
> Four excellent characters—O, that marrowless age
> Would stuff the hollow bones with damn'd desires
> And 'stead of heat, kindle infernal fires
> Within the spendthrift veins of a dry duke,
> A parch'd and juiceless luxur. O God!—one
> That has scarce blood enough to live upon,
> And he to riot it like a son and heir?
> O' the thought of that
> Turns my abused heart-strings into fret.
> Thou sallow picture of my poison'd love,
> My study's ornament, thou shell of death,
> Once the bright face of my bethothed lady,
> When life and beauty naturally fill'd out
> These ragged imperfections,
> When two heaven-pointed diamonds were set
> In those unsightly rings—then 'twas a face
> So far beyond the artificial shine
> Of any woman's bought complexion,
> That the uprightest man (if such there be
> That sin but seven times a day) broke custom
> And made up eight with looking after her.
>
> (I.i.1-25)

[14] Quotations are from *The Revenger's Tragedy*, ed. R. A. Foakes (The Revels Plays, Cambridge, Mass., 1966).

Tourneur, Middleton, Webster, Ford

Vindice's opening soliloquy, in which he holds the skull of his murdered love and comments upon the procession in dumb-show of Vice-like antagonists, immediately thrusts us back into an older dramatic world. With its personifications, *exempla* and *sententiae*, its didactic orientation toward the audience, and its use of a visual aid to bring home the moral point, the speech clearly links him with the preaching virtues of the morality tradition adduced by Salingar. We are indeed very much within the dramatic mode we have already seen to lie behind Hamlet's "Look here upon this picture, and on this," as Vindice contrasts the former "life and beauty" of his beloved's face with its present decay.

Our demonstration of the morality basis of the play is barely under way, however, when a curious resemblance to another model begins to make itself felt. *The Revenger's Tragedy* immediately evokes not only the morality models it shares with *Hamlet*, but the Shakespearean play itself, through which those older models now seem to be mediated. Vindice moralizing upon his bethothed's skull is not only a morality Virtue didactically contrasting the beauty that mirrors inward purity with the beauty that masks common corruption, but Hamlet wittily meditating upon Yorick's skull. This sense of *déjà vu* is compounded by a sense of *déjà entendu*, as Vindice's language repeatedly presses close to Hamlet's only to draw back while still remaining within earshot of it. Vindice's word-picture of his beloved's living eyes, for example, as "two heaven-pointed diamonds" still faintly echoes Hamlet's word-picture of Gertrude's former husband's "eye like Mars [and] station like the herald Mercury / New lighted on a heaven-kissing hill" (*Hamlet*, III.iv.58-60). Vindice's indictment of "the artificial shine / Of any woman's bought complexion" and of fat folks' "costly three-piled flesh worn off / As bare as this" echoes less faintly Hamlet's earlier indictments of cosmetic art to Ophelia (III.i.144-146) and his words later in the graveyard scene: "Now get you to my lady's chamber, and tell her, let her paint an inch thick, to this favor she must come" (v.i. 194-196). (Compare too Vindice's later address to the skull

"Jacobean Decadence"

in what will become the Duke's graveyard: "Does every proud and self-affecting dame / Camphor her face for this?" [III.v.84-85].) Nor are Vindice's recollections of Hamlet's language confined to his opening soliloquy; they pervade the entire play:

> And therfore I'll put on that knave for once,
> And be a right man then, a man o' th' world,
> Brother, I'll be that strange-composed fellow.
>   (I.i.93-96; cf. *Hamlet*, I.v.171; III.i.111-115)

> For since my worthy father's funeral
> My life's unnatural to me, e'en compell'd
> As if I liv'd now when I should be dead.
>   (I.i.119-121; cf. *Hamlet*, II.ii.303ff, 209-219)

> *Duke.* My teeth are eaten out....
> *Vind.* Then those that did eat are eaten.
>   (III.v.161-163; cf. *Hamlet*, IV.iii.17-21)

Other echoes could be cited, but these are sufficient to suggest that Vindice is a "strange-composed fellow" in more ways than he means, a composite of the preaching Virtues of the morality, who are his ultimate antecedents, and of Hamlet as well, who provides his more immediate inspiration. The dependence of *The Revenger's Tragedy* on morality tradition is, in fact, inseparable from its dependence on *Hamlet*.[15]

Nowhere is the play's morality derivation clearer, for example, than in its domestic subplot of Vindice's dealings with his mother and sister. These episodes are so stylized, programmatic, and tangential to the main action of revenge that we might well be tempted to regard them, in the spirit of Eliot's remarks on the subplot in Heywood, as expendable, at worst an obtrusion on the structure of the play of Tourneur's morbid preoccupation with sexuality, or at best a "fossil" or "survival" of the bare morality technique that

---

[15] A useful, though by no means complete, list of parallels is compiled by Donald Joseph McGinn, *Shakespeare's Influence on the Drama of his Age Studied in* Hamlet (New Brunswick, 1938), pp. 102-104.

is more successfully adapted in the main action. Yet for all its overt recreation of morality conventions of trial and testing, the domestic subplot is also an expanded reenactment of Hamlet's homiletic encounters with Gertrude in the closet scene and Ophelia in the nunnery scene. The parallelism becomes explicit in its final scene, when Vindice works his mother's conversion from vice after threatening her at dagger-point:

> *Grat.* What means my sons? What, will you murder me?
>
> . . . .
>
> Am I not your mother?
>
> . . . .
>
> O you heavens,
> Take this infectious spot out of my soul.
>
> (IV.iv.2-51)

As in earlier Elizabethan tragedies, the subplot makes explicit an older program of action that remains implicit in the main plot. In this instance, however, Vindice's situation and behavior are actually much more closely modeled on Hamlet's than on those of the morality virtues who lie behind Hamlet. Whereas those older figures speak and act out of an unquestionable moral authority and a prescribed moral design, the latter-day revenger has the problem of reestablishing in his own right that authoritative role and design which had formerly been a dramatic given. Both Hamlet's and Vindice's excursions into domestic morality drama may thus be seen as a kind of trial run for their larger program of redress. Vindice follows Hamlet in executing the moral prerogatives of a son toward his family as reinforcement on the way to executing the more dubious moral prerogatives of a self-styled heir and namesake to the older figure of God's Vengeance toward the world at large, "this villainous dukedom, vex'd with sin" (v.i.6), as Vindice styles it. In the hands of the latter-day revenger, morality begins at home in order that it may end, in a kind of revenger's Virgilian progression, at court. Vindice calls attention to the coherence of his career as a moral artist at the

"Jacobean Decadence"

end, when he proudly sums up his accomplishments in order of magnitude: "Our mother turn'd, our sister true; / We die after a nest of dukes. Adieu" (v.iii.124-125).

If *The Revenger's Tragedy* contains within it a moral structure as clear and firm as that of the morality play or even *Hamlet,* one to which the protagonist attempts to conform his own action, why then should the play remain so morally precarious? The answer, I would suggest, lies in Vindice's self-abandonment to the theatricality inherent in the revenger's role and the revenge form in so far as they entail a revival or imitation of an older, authoritative figure and structure of divine justice. Vindice positively exults in the theatrical flair he exhibits in fashioning an action that he self-consciously styles a "tragedy" and a justice that is nothing if not "poetic":

> *Vind.* Now to my tragic business; look you brother,
> I have not fashion'd this only for show
> And useless property; no, it shall bear a part
> E'en in it own revenge. This very skull,
> Whose mistress the duke poison'd, with this drug,
> The mortal curse of the earth, shall be reveng'd
> In the like strain, and kiss his lips to death.
> . . . .
>
> *Hipp.* Brother, I do applaud thy constant vengeance,
> The quaintness of thy malice, above thought.
>
> (III.v.99-109)

> When the bad bleeds, then is the tragedy good.
>
> (III.v.205)

> *Vind.* No power is angry when the lustful die;
> When thunder claps, heaven likes the tragedy.
>
> (v.iii.46-47)

> *Vind.* We may be bold to speak it now; 'twas somewhat witty carried, though we say it. 'Twas we two murdered him.
> *Ant.* You two?
> *Vind.* None else, i' faith, my lord; nay, 'twas well manag'd.
>
> (v.iii.96-100)

Tourneur, Middleton, Webster, Ford

The more he applauds his own plotting as an approximation of the perfect logic and economy of God's, the more he undermines his claim to ethical integrity. For poetic justice is not the same thing as divine justice, but at best an imitation and at worst a parody or mockery of it. Moreover, he simultaneously and unwittingly associates himself and his art with the Vices of the play, who have been busy with their own parallel plotting for revenge and advancement in a similar vein of grim humor. This radical moral ambivalence of the revenger-artist is figured precisely in Vindice's eager doubling as Piato, who moves with perfect ease among the plots of the Vices, in his staging of the masque of murderers in which he becomes visually indistinguishable from the other assassins, and in his self-congratulation on his wit at the end, which now turns explicitly into the self-condemnation it has implicitly been all along. The "tragedy" so proudly wrought by the revenger is inseparable from the tragedy that befalls the revenger, both meanings having been present from the start in the play's title.

What distinguishes Vindice from Hamlet, his immediate model in the poetics of revenge, is the degree to which he exceeds even Hamlet in his abandonment to the theatricality inherent in the role they share. For Hamlet too had been given to shaping plots in imitation of divine justice, particularly through the earlier acts. His decision to refrain from killing Claudius until he is in an act of sin—"Then trip him, that his heels may kick at heaven" (III.iii.93)—or his designs on Rosencrantz and Guildenstern—"For 'tis the sport to have the enginer / Hoist with his own petar. . . . / O, 'tis most sweet / When in one line two crafts directly meet" (III.iv.207-211)—anticipate Vindice at his most playful and murderous. Even after Hamlet's return from England, when he has renounced the willfull imposition of poetic justice on his world through "deep plots" of his own devising in favor of the prior and imminent justice of "a divinity that shapes our ends," even then Hamlet can hardly resist trying his own hand. It is finally Hamlet who shapes Claudius' end in an extravaganza of stabbing and poisoning

"Jacobean Decadence"

and punning designed to underscore the perfect symmetry of punishment to this incestuous poisoner's crimes: "The point envenomed too? / Then venom, to thy work. . . . / Drink off this potion. Is thy union here? / Follow my mother" (v.ii.310-315). This is poetic justice with a vengeance, even if Hamlet no longer claims to be its author. His attempt to repudiate his former theatricality is surely compromised, if not altogether contradicted, by the irresistible theatricality of his last fling.

For all their similarity, however, it is precisely Hamlet's recognition and attempted repudiation of his own theatricality that distinguishes him and his play from Vindice and his. By co-opting even heavenly thunder to his own design and making it into applause, by taking Antonio's judgment at the end as an occasion for more theatrical bravado, Vindice ultimately refuses to recognize any higher authority or truer authenticity than his own theatrical actions, which in his view have been perfectly assimilated to God's and constitute no usurpation of them. The continuing critical debate over whether there is or is not providential control at work in the play will no doubt go on, only because Vindice's theatrical control is so unyielding and preemptive. The play remains enclosed within a theatricality that converts such internal moral judgment as Antonio's into further theatricality, thus denying the characteristic Shakespearean convention of repudiating art so as to create the illusion of life and open the door from within to an ethical criticism. After following and embellishing Hamlet's theatrical recreation of an older model of conduct throughout, Vindice departs from his example in his own refusal to question the validity of the attempt to recreate that older role in the first place. By so doing, Vindice sacrifices the distinctly Shakespearean authenticity of acknowledged limitation achieved by Hamlet, but gains a new and un-Shakespearean, an almost Marlovian, authenticity of uncompromised selfhood.

In the case of *The Revenger's Tragedy*, the older model

against which Tourneur's vision is defined in its distinctiveness and originality is finally not the morality play, which now exists at two removes from it, but *Hamlet*. The apparent moral disorientation of Tourneur's play thus arises as a function of its transvaluative relation to a play that itself stands in a transvaluative relation to morality tradition. The importance of this point is that it may enable us to account for the changed nature of Jacobean tragedy in genuine literary-historical terms, that is, without recourse to the crude organicism or compulsive psychologism that underlies the concept of Jacobean decadence. If *The Revenger's Tragedy* is not atypical, it might be possible to argue that such modifications of Elizabethan practice as appear in the work of the Jacobeans are deliberate, controlled, and self-conscious, in sum, are *artistic* in the fullest sense of the term, and are conditioned by forces that are a constitutive impulse of literature itself and therefore recurrent in literary history. When we ask ourselves, what then is this new factor, ignored or obscured in most accounts of Jacobean tragedy, that conditions the poetic situation—in contradistinction to the historical situation—of Tourneur or Webster so as to differentiate it in kind from Shakespeare's, there is really only one possible answer: Shakespeare himself. The existence of Shakespeare as an inescapable presence within the poetic consciousness of the popular dramatists who succeed him is so obvious that it is not really surprising that it is rarely taken up directly as a literary-historical issue. When it is acknowledged, it is done obliquely in the form of a naive critical didacticism by which Webster or Ford is rebuked for lacking Shakespeare's undoubted virtues, or of an idealistic literary historicism in which Shakespeare is conceived of as a master whose benign and therapeutic influence is, alas, imperfectly understood or absorbed by his wayward and slightly retarded pupils. We have always been aware, that is, of Shakespeare's central significance for the playwrights who follow him, but we

"Jacobean Decadence"

state that significance under the misleading guise of strictures and platitudes, of accidental judgments, casual slaughters, and purposes mistook fallen on the inventors' heads.

That Shakespeare's followers understood the nature of his inspiration and its implications for their own art only too well will be the argument of the balance of this essay. This argument is facilitated by the weakening in recent years of the myth that Shakespeare went relatively unappreciated in his own time, by both audiences and his fellow playwrights, and remained overshadowed by Jonson throughout the seventeenth century.[16] Indeed, how could it be otherwise?

[16] The case for the preeminence of Jonson and Fletcher over Shakespeare is made by G. E. Bentley, *Shakespeare and Jonson: Their Reputations in the Seventeenth Century Compared* (Chicago, 1945), and *The Jacobean and Caroline Stage* (Oxford, 1941-56). Bentley's conclusions are convincingly refuted by David Frost, *The School of Shakespeare* (Cambridge, 1968), pp. 1-22. It is worth noting in this connection that the theory of formal exhaustion following upon the work of a major poet proposed by T. S. Eliot in his essays on Milton was anticipated by three centuries in Leonard Digges' tribute to Shakespeare prefixed to the First Folio:

> This Booke,
> When Brasse and Marble fade, shall make thee looke
> Fresh to all Ages: when Posteritie
> Shall loath what's new, thinke all is prodegie [*i.e.*, "monstrosity"]
> That is not Shake-speares. . . .
> . . . .
> Nor shall I e're beleeve, or thinke thee dead
> (Though mist) untill our bankrout Stage be sped
> (Impossible) with some new straine to out-do
> Passions of Juliet, and her Romeo. . . .
> . . . .
> Till these, till any of thy Volumes rest
> Shall with more fire, more feeling be exprest. . . .

The insistence of Digges, Jonson, and other contemporaries on Shakespeare's "feeling" and "naturalness" is clearly the Elizabethan equivalent of what would later be termed "realism" or "naturalism," a goal which such playwrights as Webster explicitly assert as their own and which Shakespeare is generally felt to have achieved.

Tourneur, Middleton, Webster, Ford

Poetic genius of the magnitude of Shakespeare's cannot be ignored or repressed by those who take their own poetic vocation seriously, precisely because it puts even more deeply into question the possibility, at all times precarious, of their own art. It must be acknowledged and addressed, not merely in the occasional form of prefaces and eulogies, but from within the very art whose distinctive existence it endangers. That Shakespeare is the single most potent and dangerous influence on the Jacobean drama is no accident. Some playwrights may indeed borrow situations, plots, characters, lines from Shakespeare's plays casually and superficially, out of convenience or fashion or uninventiveness, in the spirit in which T. S. Eliot says Heywood includes a subplot in *A Woman Killed with Kindness*, "because it is required to fill out the play." Such playwrights, like Chettle or even Massinger, are of little more than antiquarian interest today. The borrowings or, in Eliot's more accurate term "thefts," of those other Jacobeans who remain of vital interest, far from being casual and superficial, are essential to the plays they "fill out," as we have seen the subplot to actually be in Heywood. For Webster, Ford, Middleton-Tourneur, the ghost of Shakespeare must be conjured up as a presence, subsumed as a convention within their work, in order that his forbidding influence may be exorcised and his mimetic monopoly broken. Shakespeare would thus become for his Jacobean successors the necessary structural foil that medieval dramatic convention had been within the work of Shakespeare and the Elizabethans.

To test this hypothesis let us turn to the work of the Jacobean playwright most often included in "the school of Shakespeare" and to that play of his most often cited for its Shakespearean quality: Thomas Middleton's *Changeling* (1622-24). The tragedy with which it has come to be associated is *Macbeth*, largely on the basis of its protagonist's hardening to a self-chosen evil, its simultaneous movement of outward success and inward or spiritual fall, and

"Jacobean Decadence"

its self-righting moral universe within which evil inevitably destroys itself.[17] Though all these analogies are highly questionable, based as they are on a fundamentally bland and moralistic reading of *Macbeth* and Shakespearean tragedy, the play does indeed echo *Macbeth* as early as in its first three lines. Yet the case for Shakespearean influence on *The Changeling* is stronger and more interesting when *Othello* is recognized as its primary model. The twice-used epithet "honest De Flores" should be enough to alert us to the presence of *Othello* somewhere in the imaginative vicinity of the play, and on closer scrutiny it becomes clear that Shakespeare's play is nothing less than the substructure on which Middleton's rests. What is its trio of principals, Alsemero, Beatrice and De Flores, but Othello, Desdemona, and Iago in reprise, and its triangular action but a replotting of *Othello*? The adultery contrived by Iago and imagined by Othello now becomes real, as the noble Alsemero is betrayed by a new and changed Desdemona and another Iago. The final scene of *The Changeling*, in which Alsemero exposes Beatrice and De Flores, distinctly parallels in language and incident the brothel scene and denouement of *Othello*, though here Alsemero's accusations are wholly accurate. Even such secondary characters as Beatrice's father Vermandero and her maid Diaphanta recall their Shakespearean counterparts, the former a more permissive Brabantio and the latter a looser Emilia. *The Changeling* contains a rewriting of *Othello* at its core.

How does Middleton manage this revision so as to endow it with a dramatic life of its own and prevent it from be-

[17] The influence of Shakespeare's villains on the characterization of De Flores was first suggested by A. W. Ward, *A History of English Dramatic Literature* (London, 1875), vol. II, p. 82, and the similarity between the appearance of Alonzo's ghost in v.i. and Banquo's ghost by Hugo Jung, *Das Verhältnis Thomas Middletons zu Shakespeare* (Leipzig, 1904), pp. 84-87. See especially Helen Gardner, "Milton's Satan and the Theme of Damnation in Elizabethan Tragedy," *Essays and Studies*, 1 (1948), 42-61. References in my text are to *The Changeling*, ed. N. W. Bawcutt (The Revels Plays, Cambridge, Mass., 1958).

Tourneur, Middleton, Webster, Ford

coming a dull echo of Shakespeare? Just as the versions of medieval drama Shakespeare subsumes within his plays are really subversions of that older drama, so the version of Shakespeare Middleton now subsumes within his is also a subversion, a foil or parody that enables him to define his own dramatic vision by defining what it is not. In *The Changeling*, this foil takes the form, not of a subplot or an internal play, but of a loose-fitting frame that opens and closes the play on a distinctly Shakespearean note. We recognize, for example, in the rhetoric of love with which Alsemero opens the play the same impulse to allegorize his experience that we have already seen in Othello ("It gives me wonder great as my content . . ."):

> The place is holy, so is my intent:
> I love her beauties to the holy purpose,
> And that methinks, admits comparison
> With man's first creation, the place blest,
> And is his right home back, if he achieve it.
> The church hath first begun our interview,
> And that's the place must join us into one,
> So there's beginning and perfection too.
>
> (I.i.5-12)

Othello-like as the speech is, however, it has a quality that distinguishes Alsemero's voice from Othello's even as it recalls it. Whereas Othello lays his whole being on the line with every metaphor he hazards, Alsemero hedges his linguistic bets in simile and qualification: "admits comparison," "methinks," "if he achieve it" are not constructions that come readily to a character for whom language is a magical force able to conjure its reference into being. There is also a syllogistic, almost legalistic, movement to Alsemero's speech that is quite alien to Othello's, the logicality of a nature that does not stand or fall, as Othello's does, on the presence or absence of absolute faith. Though these subtle differences eventually prove crucial, the Alsemero who opens the play is a reasonable facsimile of Othello, a

"Jacobean Decadence"

romantic wanderer about to exchange his unhoused, free condition for a love invested with transcendent meaning. The resemblance is certainly strong enough to cause us to view all that follows in the reflected light of Shakespeare's play.

That these initial recollections of *Othello* are not merely local or fortuitous is evident from the fact that Middleton repeatedly places Alsemero in Othello's position, all the while maintaining a certain resemblance and a certain sense of difference between their respective conduct. When, for example, he hears his bride's chastity impugned by his trusted companion, Alsemero does not seize her accuser by the throat, grovel in madness on the stage, swear himself to a sacred vow of revenge, or demand compelling ocular proof. Instead, he calmly warns Jasperino of the gravity of his charge, sends for the virginity test "By a Chaldean taught me" (IV.ii.112)—the exoticism underscores the contrast with Othello—and pragmatically proceeds to relieve his doubts. It matters less that he is deceived in its results than that he would resort to such a mechanistic test of virginity in the first place, something his Shakespearean original would never have done even if he had had one available. Similarly, in the final scene, when Alsemero takes up the role of prosecutor and judge, he does so with none of Othello's controlled but compulsive fury. He is content to elicit the truth from Beatrice, paint a vivid word-picture of the adulterers in hell (perhaps derived from Othello's own self-condemnations), and leave them to their posthumous punishment. By the end of the scene, Alsemero has actually relaxed into the choric role, usually reserved in Shakespeare for such tragic subordinates as Lodovico, Horatio, and Edgar, of summing up recent events and proclaiming the reestablishment of social and moral order:

> Justice hath so right
> The guilty hit, that innocence is quit
> By proclamation, and may joy again.
> (v.iii.185-187)

Tourneur, Middleton, Webster, Ford

From the theological reductions with which he opens the play to the pietistic reductions with which he closes it, Alsemero is consistently presented as a prosaic and deintensified Othello.

This is not to suggest, however, that *The Changeling* is simply a deromanticization of *Othello*, as if it merely carried a stage further the demystification of exalted role-playing we have seen already at work in Shakespeare's play, though Middleton's play does indeed contain a movement of this kind. It is implicit in his characterization of Alsemero and quite explicit in that of De Flores, one of whose main activities within the play is to demystify the illusions of others. The famous lines, for example, in which he deflates Beatrice's pretensions to maidenly virtue—"A woman dipp'd in blood and talk of modesty?"; "Y're the deed's creature; by that name / You lost your first condition" (III.iv.126, 137-138)—reach much further than the particular deed of blood to which they refer. For De Flores' reference is to the more widespread scandal of human carnality that is as old as original sin and that renders all exalted human role-playing—not just Beatrice's belated pretensions to the modesty of a Desdemona—something of a mockery. Unlike his Shakespearean prototype, De Flores indulges in no melodramatic cultivation of evil, no pluming up of the will in knavery, for he harbors no self-aggrandizing illusions even about himself—not about his ugliness, his lust for Beatrice, or the price that will have to be paid: "my life I rate at nothing" (III.iv.149). Yet this demystification of the human impulse to self-etherealization and of the codes of social morality that underlie and reinforce it—particularly as they are projected in Shakespearean drama—represents only half of Middleton's dramatic project, a kind of clearing the stage of older Shakespearean props in order that a new and distinctive drama may be mounted.

For Middleton does indeed mount his own highly un-Shakespearean, indeed anti-Shakespearean, drama out of the ruins of the relationship between Alsemero and Beatrice

"Jacobean Decadence"

and centers it on the developing relationship between De Flores and Beatrice at the heart of the play. The heroism and romance that have been emptied from the former relationship are now displaced into the latter:

> I'm forced to love thee now,
> 'Cause thou provid'st so carefully for my honour.
> (v.i.47-48)

> How rare is that man's speed!
> How heartily he serves me! His face loathes one,
> But look upon his care, who would not love him?
> The east is not more beauteous than his service.
> (v.i.69-72)

All the high romanticism of *Romeo and Juliet*, as well as *Othello*, is evoked—and travestied—in Beatrice's line. De Flores has become the "wondrous necessary man" who enables Beatrice to preserve her romantic illusions even after her "fall." Yet it is by no means stretching the point to say that theirs, in the depth and solicitude of the bond that grows between them, is the true marriage of the play, that of Beatrice and Alsemero the sham. It now makes perfect dramatic sense for Middleton to reassign in the closing scene Othello's final heroic gestures and assertions, not to the moralizing Alsemero, but to the De Flores who, with his coarse eloquence and decisive action, has upstaged him. What critics describe, quite accurately, as Beatrice's hardening into sin can also be described, with equal accuracy, as a softening into love, as a preservation of innocence beyond her ostensible fall, a radical recovery of what De Flores terms her "first condition." Similarly, to be scandalized by her repeated protestations of innocence in the final scene and regard them as the final measure of her "hypocrisy" is to adopt the narrowly moralistic viewpoint of Alsemero, which we all no doubt have a vested interest in endorsing. But to do so is also to underinterpret the depth of her latest self-dramatization, for hers is no conventional hypocrisy and

Tourneur, Middleton, Webster, Ford

no superficial role-playing. The innocence she maintains is of course not ethical or legal, but is an esthetic innocence not unlike that uncompromising acting out of an older and purer role displayed by the very Shakespearean heroines Beatrice now hollowly echoes, however lacking it is in the moral justification that would gain it our willing credit. In the counterplay of De Flores and Beatrice, Middleton has opened a new appeal from Shakespeare's moral fictions to something closer to the passionate amorality of nature.

We seem to have educed a principle of structural differentiation that may begin to account not only for the changeling Middleton has wrought on *Othello*, but for the larger change that occurs from Elizabethan and Shakespearean to Jacobean tragedy. In Shakespeare and the Elizabethans there is always substantial congruity between their morality substructures and the more modern and naturalistic actions based upon them, however imaginatively the latter action revises the former. Antony and Cleopatra's rewriting of a morality action follows closely upon and converges toward the final transcendence of the former, even if its movement is now toward the transcendence of erotic, rather than ascetic, love. Othello's final heroic extenuation, in its imaginative union of self-condemnation and self-redemption, remains guided by the conventions of closure handed down by morality tradition. Similarly, in *The Changeling* the imaginative revision centered on De Flores and Beatrice retains as its point of departure, not so much any traditional morality action, as the pseudo-Shakespearean tragedy of Alsemero and Beatrice, in so far as it is a negative and amoral reconstruction of that model. For even though Beatrice ultimately accepts her society's condemnation of her, De Flores has put himself well beyond the reach both of medieval moral sanctities and Shakespearean moral and social sanctions. From his shocking mutilation of Alonso's corpse, through his dismissals of an anachronistic ghost, to his unashamed self-assertion at the end, De Flores maintains his existence outside the

"Jacobean Decadence"

moral and dramatic decorum that even Shakespeare's villains sooner or later acknowledge. For De Flores, unlike Beatrice, never relapses into Edmund's self-justifications, or Iago's last-ditch efforts at concealment, or Macbeth's sense of loss, though we need these models to measure his difference from them. But it is only by suppressing the amoral vitality of De Flores and unduly privileging the moralistic blandness of his foil Alsemero or the final repentance of Beatrice that the play can be said to inhabit a Shakespearean universe. It is against Middleton's explicit displacement of his play's center of imaginative intensity away from the social morality of its Shakespearean foil that critics repeatedly assert its connection with a dramatic universe from which it has taken leave from the start.

In the ongoing history of mimesis not even the monumental achievement of Shakespeare is sacred. It too is subject to the same imaginative subversion of prior convention that conditions every new and authentic representation of experience. Middleton has taken over the moral orientation of Shakespearean tragedy that remains as a by-product of its own subversion of morality forms, identified that moralism as a blind spot in Shakespeare's vision of life, and thereby opened a new appeal from art to nature, from archaism to modernity, and from morality to mimesis. The point is not that Shakespeare is or is not moralistic, but that his work can be made to seem moralistic in so far as it is still mediated by morality tradition, and can therefore be made over into a new point of departure for a mimetic revisionism forever seeking to do away with all such mediations. To put it another way, Middleton has taken over and taken further the romantic element implicit in Shakespearean tragedy, the subjective truth of the hero's experience, and pitted it against the pious or conservative element also implicit there, the social or public morality that opposes subjective or heroic truth in the interest of order and continuity. The fact that Middleton does at least retain both elements of the Shakespearean synthesis, however fundamentally he upsets the Shakespearean balance, allows those critics responsive to the energy of his revision but respectful toward traditional morality a way out of their dilemma by praising Middleton for his Shakespeareanism when he has actually put it into question from within.

Webster's revision of Shakespeare, in contrast to Middleton's, is at once more obvious and more subtle, more elusive yet farther-reaching. It is not so much a matter of his tipping the Shakespearean balance in favor of either the romantic or the pious side as of his emptying *both* sides of that balance, the pious and romantic alike. As a result, Webster is not usually seen as the direct descendant of Shakespeare that Middleton is, but more often as a problematic and wayward disciple, though the precise nature of his perversity is by no means unanimously agreed upon. Although most critics agree that Webster's dramatic universe is morally uncentered or disoriented compared to Shakespeare's, fewer would agree that his presentation of romantic and heroic self-assertion is also fundamentally anti-Shakespearean. On the contrary, most would argue that it is precisely this side of Webster, as epitomized in the pathetic grandeur of the Duchess of Malfi and the dazzling self-dramatization of Vittoria and Flamineo, that lends Webster whatever Shakespearean quality, usually equated with dramatic excellence, his work possesses. Yet if the moral uncertainty widely observed in Webster's plays can be traced to his deliberate deconstruction of the pious side of Shakespeare's achievement, it may well be that the theatrical shiftiness also frequently pointed out is the result of an analogous deconstruction of the romantic or subjective aspect of Shakespearean drama as well. Webster's revision of Shakespeare, in sum, may be more consistent and coherent than is generally thought.

It is at once clear that Webster's tragedies, whatever the source of their moral indeterminacy, do not present us with a moral vacuum. In *The White Devil*, for example,

"Jacobean Decadence"

the mantle of traditional virtue is assumed by one character after another as the play proceeds, so that there is scarcely a scene in which someone is not preaching at the others in the manner of the Virtue-figures of the morality play itself. At the outset, we hear Antonelli and Gasparo advise "penance" and "virtue" to the "justly doom'd" Lodovico. In the second scene, it is Cornelia who, overhearing the verbal foreplay of Bracciano, Vittoria, and Flamineo, announces herself in a style that indentifies her with a long line of preaching virtues: "Woe to light hearts—they still forerun our fall" (I.ii.269). Next it is Francisco, Monticelso, and Isabella admonishing Bracciano, in the manner of Shakespeare's Romans, to end his degrading infatuation with Vittoria and return to princely virtue and marital duty. Throughout the play, Webster thus keeps before us a running moral commentary on events, a frame of traditional moral reference invoked by even the most deviant characters. The fact that this moral perspective is largely rejected by a predominantly vicious or venal world has suggested to several commentators the poetics of satire, a genre that thrives on the proliferation of examples of unheeded virtue. This association of the plays with satire would make the problem of their moral disintegration an easy one, were it not for the difficulty of locating an authoritative moral spokesman in whom to believe and against whom to measure the deviance of others. For even the most apparently virtuous characters are open to suspicion. It has been pointed out that in *The White Devil* both Cornelia and Marcello benefit from the largesse of the Bracciano they condemn, despite their protestations of honest poverty.[18] Monticelso's motives in casting himself as the guardian of justice and morality before and during Vittoria's trial are always murky, and his possession of a "general catalogue of knaves"

---

[18] By John Russell Brown, ed., *The White Devil* (The Revels Plays, London, 1960), pp. lii-liv. Quotations in my text are from this edition, and from *The Duchess of Malfi*, ed. John Russell Brown (The Revels Plays, London, 1964).

raises questions as to his purposes in keeping it. In *The Duchess of Malfi*, too, the moral stature of the Duchess is undermined by the secrecy of her marriage, her disregard for her public reputation, and her subterfuge of undertaking a pilgrimage to Loretto as a means of being reunited with her husband. Even the loyal and benign Delio's claim to moral authority is compromised by his dubious association with the Cardinal's mistress Julia. The best in Webster's world, as has often been pointed out, are morally distinguished only in degree, and not in kind, from the worst. The question remains—and it is not helped by appeal to the norms of satire—why plays in which morality is everywhere should be so morally indeterminate.

The answer lies not in the decline or decay of morality, either within or outside Webster's plays, but in what might be termed the theatricalization of morality. Roles, postures, speeches, and gestures once identified with an authentic and un-self-conscious virtue—theatricality being the exclusive preserve of vice—now become the common repertory of virtue and vice alike and are put on and off at will. In the third scene of *The White Devil*, for example, we find Isabella mounting one last attempt to regain her strayed husband through a device of theatrical indirection. She will absolve Bracciano of all blame for their separation by pretending to be a shrewish and vindictive wife:

> No my dear lord, you shall have present witness
> How I'll work peace between you [and Francisco],—
>   I will make
> Myself the author of your cursed vow—
> I have some cause to do it, you have none,—
> Conceal it I beseech you, for the weal
> Of both your kingdoms, that you wrought the means
> Of such a separation, let the fault
> Remain with my supposed jealousy,—
> And think with what a piteous and rent heart,
> I shall perform this sad ensuing part.
>   (II.i.216-225)

"Jacobean Decadence"

To maintain her wifely virtue Isabella takes on the role of vice, enacting it so successfully as to deceive Francisco into believing that it is her own willfulness rather than Bracciano's that has caused the rift between them. The effect of her ruse is not only to blur or conceal her psychological motives—does she act in order to preserve peace between her brother and husband, as she says, or in the hope of winning back Bracciano through a show of self-sacrifice?—but to compromise the very moral probity she claims to exemplify. In Webster generally, virtue compromises itself by adopting the theatrical mode of existence of its conventional opponent. Thus the Duchess of Malfi tells Antonio, amid her own highly contrived scene of mock-temptation and marriage, that we "Are forc'd to . . . leave the path / Of simple virtue, which was never made / To seem the thing it is not" (I.i.445-448). Webster consistently reveals the theatrical nature that pious roles have in common with romantic roles and that renders the former no more stable or trustworthy than the latter. If Isabella can so easily shift into the Cleopatra-like role of the vindictive shrew, how can we accept the Desdemona-like identity of patient virtue she claims as hers? The tension that is always present between heart-feeling ("A piteous and rent heart") and part-playing ("this sad, ensuing part") is not resolved or relaxed but heightened by the skill with which she brings off her scene, just as the divergence in meaning between the echoing words themselves is underscored by the facility of their rhyme. Even Webster's quasi-virtuous characters do not so much act out of their presumably moral natures as act their allegedly moral natures out, putting them into question in the process.

Webster's difference from Shakespeare in this respect is significant. It is not that the Virtue-figures in Shakespeare are above or beyond role-playing; on the contrary, Cordelia, in her refusal to lie, recant, or recriminate throughout *Lear*, and Desdemona, in her readiness to exonerate her persecutor in the final scene of *Othello*, are playing one of the

Tourneur, Middleton, Webster, Ford

oldest roles of all. The difference is that they bring a histrionic innocence to their role-playing, comparable perhaps, though certainly not equivalent, to that total identification with their parts which folk actors are sometimes said to grow into in the course of performing latter-day revivals of the passion play, and which we have already seen reproduced in parodistic form in Beatrice's self-conviction of innocence in *The Changeling*. In Shakespearean tragedy, this histrionic innocence is ultimately reinforced and ratified by the society that surrounds the characters who display it, however belatedly the tragic hero himself joins in that ratification. Cordelia and Desdemona are seen to be precious and unique not because they play their roles well, but because they refuse to acknowledge that they play at all. Shakespeare's tragic societies subsist and survive on the saving fiction that moral authenticity is possible, in spite of or perhaps because of the passing of the exemplar who incarnates it. Edgar's curious line at the end of *Lear*, "Speak what we feel, not what we ought to say," makes into a categorical imperative Cordelia's ethical and linguistic stance in the opening scene. In Webster, however, no such fiction of authenticity is allowed to survive. Even those characters with some claim to virtue, such as Isabella, are theatrically self-conscious, and those who are not, such as Cornelia, have attention called to the theatrically of their postures by the characters around them. Webster's creatures inhabit a universe in which it is impossible to avoid consciousness of the theatricality of their own lives, and the moral inauthenticity it entails.

It remains to be demonstrated, however, that Webster's theatricalization of morality is not merely un-Shakespearean but anti-Shakespearean, part of a deliberate and consistent strategy of reaction to his specific influence. This could be shown through the example of Isabella, whose postures in the scene we have been examining are modeled on those of Cordelia and Desdemona, as well as Cleopatra, and in fact play the latter off against the former. We will reach further,

"Jacobean Decadence"

however, by turning to a more obvious echo of Shakespeare, one that many commentators have recognized as such: the episode of Cornelia's lament after the murder of Marcello by Flamineo. After listing the many verbal parallelisms between Cornelia's ravings and those of Lear and Ophelia, one critic observes, "There is more than a suspicion that Cornelia's madness was introduced because Webster was overwhelmed by the pathos of Lear and Ophelia. Yet this demonstrates how much the Jacobeans . . . were impressed by Shakespeare and fell back on him when it was a case of depicting and arousing emotion."[19] The assumptions here are that Webster is straining to achieve the same dramatic effects as Shakespeare, and that this common purpose conditions Webster's recourse to Shakespearean language. Another critic, attempting to show that family relationships in *The White Devil* are more an emblem of social disintegration than a vital concern in themselves, continues in the same vein: "Cornelia's motherly grief goes some way towards being an exception from this rule and no doubt Webster is here feeling his way to a realised situation; but it is significant that he has to do it through such particularly wholesale borrowings from Shakespeare."[20] Leaving aside their undertone of condescension, the clear trend of these arguments is that whatever authenticity as a dramatist Webster reveals in these scenes, and presumably elsewhere as well, is the result of his imitating Shakespeare. Faced

---

[19] Frost, *The School of Shakespeare*, p. 149. Frost's book is useful as a collection of Shakespearean echoes and parallels in the work of his successors, but seriously wanting in the theoretical and methodological sophistication necessary to make literary-historical sense of them. Even more undiscriminating is R. W. Dent, *John Webster's Borrowing* (Berkeley, 1960), which documents the received idea of Webster's plays as mosaics pieced together out of other men's writings. A suggestive treatment of the general problem is that of H. J. Oliver, "Literary Allusions in Jacobean Drama," in *Renaissance Studies in Honor of Carroll Camden* (Houston, 1974), pp. 131-140.

[20] Inga-Stina Ewbank, "Webster's Realism or, 'A Cunning Piece Wrought Perspective,'" in *John Webster*, ed. Brian Morris (London, 1970), p. 175.

with such a paradoxical conclusion, one to which the critics who unconsciously advance it would hardly assent, we might do well to retrace our steps.

That these scenes are an extended allusion to Shakespeare is beyond doubt, but there is no reason to assume that they are employed imitatively by Webster to achieve a pathos similar to that achieved by Shakespeare. On the contrary, they are handled in such a way as to undercut the familiar Shakespearean pathos even as they imitate it. The very closeness and duration of the parallelism between Cornelia's ramblings and Lear's and Ophelia's, their rhetorical repetitions and unmissable references to a feather, a looking-glass, and a series of emblematic flowers, create a tonality of fine excess, an over-allusiveness that makes Cornelia's suffering seem studied or overacted, even "literary." For Webster encourages us to maintain an esthetic distance in relation to Cornelia that Shakespeare does not allow us in relation to Lear or even Ophelia. The repeated denials, in a somewhat matter-of-fact voice, by Carlo and Hortensio of Cornelia's anguished cries that Marcello lives have no counterpart in the closing scene of *Lear*, where the voice of pathos is permitted free and uncontradicted expression. Nor has Marcello been presented as a Cordelia, despite his relative innocence within the world of the play and Cornelia's strenuous efforts to make him into one. Though he is the "virtuous" of two brothers, he lacks Edgar's redeeming good-will, and to that extent too Cordelia's highly derivative grief seems in excess of its object, all due allowance made for maternal love. When Cornelia reenters in the following scene, echoing Ophelia's distraction and funeral song almost verbatim, the esthetic distance that Webster has maintained throughout between Cornelia and us is further widened by the choric commentary around her: "Her ladyship's foolish." "Alas! her grief / Hath turn'd her child again" (v.iv.74-76). It is as if Cornelia were determined to reenact the pathos of Lear and Ophelia in a dramatic world in which pathos is not allowed unmediated

"Jacobean Decadence"

expression. We might conclude at this point that the artificial and anachronistic dimension of Cornelia's grief is a measure of how far Webster's world has fallen from Shakespeare's. But such a conclusion would be premature and nostalgic. For Webster is also drawing attention to a condition that no dramatic representation of pathos, not even Shakespeare's in so far as it is dramatic and a *re*presentation, can fully escape. By emphasizing and exaggerating in Cornelia the artificial constituent of even Shakespearean pathos, Webster has opened an imaginative space between Shakespeare and "life" which his own deliberately mock-pathetic art now fills. We are used to seeing Webster regarded as a foil to Shakespeare; but there is a compelling sense in which Shakespeare must be seen as a foil to Webster, if, paradoxically, Webster's art is to be taken on its own terms.

This making over of that which had seemed pure and spontaneous into something conspicuously artful and derivative is not confined to the mock-pious and mock-pathetic side of Webster's art but extends to the allegedly romantic side of it as well. Both *The White Devil* and *The Duchess of Malfi* are built of and built toward moments in which their protagonists strike quasi-Shakespearean stances in asserting a selfhood that elicits an undeniable admiration, however flagrantly it violates social and moral norms. Consider, for example, the arraignment of Vittoria at the center of *The White Devil*. There, a series of Biblical and allegorical images are superimposed in morality fashion upon Vittoria by her prosecutors—the serpent, the whore, the devils Adultery and Murder—to which we are supposed to mark her resemblance. "If the devil," sums up Monticelso, "Did ever take good shape, behold his picture" (III.ii.216-217). Far from denoting her truly and essentially, however, these stagy abstractions enable Vittoria to define herself against them in terms of a womanly frailty that seems convincing by contrast: "These are but feigned shadows of my evils. / Terrify babes, my lord, with painted devils, / I am past such needless palsy" (III.ii.146-148). The

Tourneur, Middleton, Webster, Ford

Shakespearean allusion is not accidental. Throughout the scene, Vittoria surpasses Lady Macbeth herself in histrionic bravado and sustains the role of Shakespeare's own calumniated heroines, notably Hermione at a similar trial two years earlier. But Vittoria's casting herself as a Shakespearean innocent, though it wins the admiration of the English ambassador present and of most viewers of the play, repeatedly calls attention to itself as a "personated" virtue and a feigned innocence. Vittoria's moment of self-presentation turns into one of imitation. Quite apart from the moral culpability of her perjured testimony, the ontological status of the self she presents is undermined by the very theatricality and imitativeness of its mode of presentation. To paraphrase Monticelso, such counterfeit selves make the existence of a "true" self oft-suspected. Will the real Vittoria Corombona please stand up?

Not even at the end of the play, at what is usually regarded as the definitive moment of death, does the "real" Vittoria stand up, and not because she refuses or is afraid to—that would make the play relatively unproblematic—but because there is no "real" Vittoria to stand up. For the deaths, not only of Vittoria but of all Webster's principal characters, are haunted by a seemingly inescapable theatricality; they do not so much die as enact their death, play out a death scene in which they are at once actors and spectators. In *The White Devil* this playing at death is underscored by the device of successive death-scenes: the first staged by Flamineo to test his sister's truth, and the second by Lodovico ostensibly in revenge for the murder of Isabella. The first or mock death scene, in which brother and sister strike alternately loyal and ruthless poses as each gains the drop on the other, might well have served as foil to the real death scene that follows, one more interlude of role-playing to point up the emergence of their more authentic selves in the face of imminent death. Yet no such authenticity does finally emerge, but only a deeper theatricality, much as in the trial scene the broad morality roles imposed

"Jacobean Decadence"

on Vittoria gave way to her own more subtle and Shakespearean role-playing, or the legalistic obscurity of Latin was abandoned only to be replaced by the less obvious concealments of the vernacular. Flamineo's dying speeches combine and caricature the black humor of Mercutio and the bravado of Othello—"O what blade is't? / A Toledo, or an English fox?" (v.vi.234-235)—while those of Vittoria imitate the imperious gaiety of Cleopatra—"Behold my breast,— / I will be waited on in death; my servant / Shall never go before me" (v.vi.216-218). It is revealing that even Vittoria's most famous, characteristic, and romantic lines—"My soul, like to a ship in a black storm, / Is driven I know not whither" (v.v.248-249), for example—can be traced back to sources in Shakespeare, in this case to one of Othello's late speeches (v.ii.268-280). And even when Webster's language is not explicitly Shakespearean—as it is not, for example, in Flamineo's final speech ("I have caught / An everlasting cold. I have lost my voice . . . Strike thunder, and strike loud to my farewell" [v.vi.270-276])—it is still a theatrically self-conscious and self-referential language, as if its speaker were imprisoned within a condition of theatricality from which death is indeed the only release, the victim of an ontological flippancy at the heart of things.

Even in *The Duchess of Malfi*, which has seemed to many the less cerebral and cold-blooded, the more heartfelt of Webster's tragedies, the emergence and very existence of an authentic selfhood is threatened by a no less pervasive theatricality. The Duchess' death scene is often cited as the locus of existential self-definition, though there is by no means agreement as to the nature of the self supposedly defined there. Her early echoes of *Richard II*—"Sit down; / Discourse to me some dismal tragedy" (IV.ii.7-8)—might suggest a parallel growth from passive victim into active protagonist, establishing a deeper regality in the process. Yet the Duchess could be conversely described as moving from tragic resistance to pathos, since her assertion of a lofty and inviolable selfhood as "Duchess of Malfi still" comes early in the scene and gives way quickly under Bosola's relentless "mortification" to the minimal identity of woman and mother, as she renounces further distinctions before death. Both these descriptions of her growth, however, lead us to expect a stable or developing self to emerge from the Duchess' actions, much as we come to perceive the hand of the director lending coherence to a theatrical production. That the Duchess does not perform at the inner direction of such a self is suggested by the very effortlessness of her improvisation of the contradictory stances of defiance and humility, of Medea-Cleopatra and Hermione, under the prompting of Bosola: "I know death hath ten thousand several doors / For men to take their exits . . . any way, for heaven-sake, / So I were out of your whispering" (IV.ii.219-223). However contradictory these roles may be or however sudden the transition from one to the other, they can be flawlessly performed precisely because of the absence of a self to impede their execution. "Who do I look like now?" she asks Cariola before her death, and the latter's answer points to the void we often say exists within the greatest actors:

> Like to your picture in the gallery,
> A deal of life in show, but none in practice;
> Or rather like some reverend monument
> Whose ruins are even pitied.
> (IV.ii.31-34)

Nor is this estrangement from a distinctive and autonomous self, which endows her actions with the detached, almost posthumous, air of an actor, a ghost, or (in another of her images) a somnambulist, unique to the Duchess. How else are we to account for Ferdinand's wrenching transformation from vindictive tyrant to repentant brother, or Bosola's sudden conversion from sadistic confessor to would-be reviver, except in terms of a radical alienation from the self that makes the dark motivations and gratuitous passions of *Measure for Measure* and *The Winter's Tale*

"Jacobean Decadence"

(which are explicitly recalled) seem almost normal? For all the principals in this play of effigies and echoes are walking shadows united finally in a common self-alienation that dooms them, as Ferdinand (echoing Leontes) says of the Duchess, to be "plagued in art" (IV.i.iii), to a state of voyeurism on their own lives, of nostalgia for the present.

Webster's difference from Shakespeare on the dramatic status of the self, dependent as it is on the internalized presence of Shakespeare, is fundamental to even the most preliminary understanding of his work. We have seen how in Shakespeare forms and roles from prior tradition are put on and taken off only to imply the existence of a selfhood just beyond the reach of prior tradition. Cleopatra's question, "Think you there was or might be such a man / As this I dreamt of?" (V.ii.94-95), is rhetorically confident of an affirmative answer, despite Dolabella's Roman skepticism. It may take plays within plays and roles beneath roles to begin to close in on the truth of the self, but that truth is always assumed to be there for the playing, available to the mechanisms of mimesis and endomimesis by which it can be at least indirectly mirrored or mocked. In Webster, by contrast, the same mechanisms that in Shakespeare's hands had led toward the establishment and definition of the self now lead only toward its *dis*establishment and *un*definition, toward the perception of its radical indeterminacy. In the conventional terminology of dramatic criticism, Shakespeare's protagonists see their way through "illusion" or "appearance" to "reality," whereas Webster's see their way through "appearance" not to "reality," but to the void within the born actor that dooms him to involuntary and joyless improvisation for the whole of his natural life: "I account this world a tedious theatre, / For I do play a part in't 'gainst my will" (*D. of M.*, IV.i.84-85). Unlike the Macbeth she echoes, who wilfully reduces himself to a walking shadow against the Shakespearean norm of fullness and vitality, the Duchess voices the Websterian norm in an altered world where shifting theatrical appear-

Tourneur, Middleton, Webster, Ford

ances are all and to which there is no alternative. A special case in Shakespeare has been made general by Webster. For he does not present opposed "realities" of theater and life, or even the theatrical dimension *of* life, but the inescapable theatricality that *is* life; not actors discovering their true or real selves, but presumably "flesh-and-blood" human beings discovering the actors that they are. The drama within Websterian tragedy consists, in sum, precisely in the discovery on the part of its principals that they cannot be the Shakespearean characters they had thought they were. It is no wonder critics approaching Webster's plays with Shakespearean expectations of self-discovery and self-authentication find so much confusion in them, since their movement from mimetic fullness to allegorical insubstantiality reverses that of their Shakespearean foils.[21]

These observations are obviously too brief and lapidary to do justice to the dramatist who, more fully than any other, faces and overcomes the menace of Shakespeare's dazzling priority. It would be even more injudicious, however, to embark so late in this abstract and brief chronicle of the tragic drama that has Shakespeare at its center upon a reinterpretation of the work of John Ford, though a few tentative remarks on Ford's relation to that tradition might not seem altogether out of place here. If there is any truth in the foregoing argument, Ford's creative dependence on Shakespeare can now be taken for granted. In his self-consciously belated chronicle play *Perkin Warbeck*, for example, Ford could scarcely have chosen a subject more evocative of Shakespeare's histories than the reign of Henry

[21] The Websterian movement toward depersonalization is enacted in the change from the Duchess' early assertion to Antonio that she is "flesh and blood, sir . . . *not* the figure cut in alabaster / Kneels at my husband's tomb" (I.i.454-455) to her acceptance of Cariola's image of her as "some reverend monument / Whose ruins are even pitied" (IV.ii.33-34). This movement carries over into the final act, where the Duchess survives in the disembodied and posthumous form of an echo, a voice emptied of personality and a sign emptied of significance.

"Jacobean Decadence"

VII, on whom Shakespeare's two tetralogies had come to rest and in whom the Shakespearean requirements for successful kingship—mastery of the art of power and some claim to the throne—are now recreated. Against the Bolingbroke-like Henry, however, Ford pits the pretender Perkin, who is sometimes said to be modelled on Richard II, but in whom a more Marlovian power to redefine reality through an unwavering role-playing and draw others into his vision is now reenacted. Ford, so to speak, plays Marlowe off against Shakespeare in a mutually destructive dialectic. As long as Perkin is around to upstage him with royal language far more magically potent then his own, Henry must seem something of "a mockery-king in state" (I.i.4), though Perkin can never fully consolidate his role and make his royal word flesh in a world where even his strongest ally is subject to a pragmatic inconstancy akin to Henry's own. In playing off Marlovian "strength of passion" against Shakespearean "threats of majesty," the play recreates the traditional strains of the Elizabethan history play while moving toward a hollow and queasy victory in which both are reduced to mere "theatres of greatness . . . / Proving their weak foundations" (Epilogue, 2-5).[22]

In this respect, *Perkin Warbeck* is very much of a piece with what is usually said to be Ford's more characteristic work, notably '*Tis Pity She's a Whore*. If *Perkin* recapitulates while demystifying the conventions of the history play, '*Tis Pity* bears a similar relation to the tradition of Elizabethan and Jacobean tragedy it concludes. There too Shakespeare is present, primarily in the form of the tragedy of forbidden love and social constraint based on *Romeo and Juliet* that the play subsumes. But so too is Marlowe in the form of Giovanni's tragedy of unfaltering Faustian defiance of the "laws of conscience and of civil use" (v.v.70). This

[22] Quotations are from *The Chronicle History of Perkin Warbeck*, ed. Peter Ure (The Revels Plays, London, 1968), and '*Tis Pity She's a Whore*, ed. N. W. Bawcutt (Regents Renaissance Drama Series, Lincoln, Nebraska, 1966).

Tourneur, Middleton, Webster, Ford

Marlovian presence once again prevents the action from conforming strictly to its Shakespearean model. In fact, by the end of *'Tis Pity*, the principals are desperately casting about among the entire repertory of the Elizabethan and Jacobean theater for roles to shore against their ruin. Soranzo becomes a degraded Othello; the Spaniard Vasques' revenge-plotting recalls that of his countryman Hieronimo and Vindice's as well; Annabella patterns herself on Middleton's falling but repentant heroines; and the Cardinal proves true to his venal Websterian prototypes. This is not the place to explore the many affiliations between Ford's play and the dramatic tradition it reconstitutes in a tissue of parodic allusion. But perhaps it is not too fanciful to suggest that Fordian tragedy is promiscuous, even incestuous, in its very conception, that the "births abortive" and "bastard brood" Ford admits the possibility of seeing in *Perkin Warbeck* (Epilogue, 7) may be identified with his work as a whole, begotten as it is out of a melancholy awareness of the embarrassment of models already in place before him. Their very existence might well seem to disinherit him of his own place within a tradition in which all imaginative positions have already been taken, relegating the playwright Ford to something of the marginal status of an incestuous or illegitimate offspring who has no rightful place within the family or social structure.

In our readings of the major Jacobeans in the light of Shakespeare, we are left with the paradox that the most original attempts to transcend Shakespeare's influence should take the form of revealing, too consistently and self-consciously to be anything but deliberate, the inescapability of his influence. But this is the form of literary history at large and cannot be avoided by the poet who would secure his place within it. The real "Jacobean decadents," in so far as that concept retains any literary-historical value, are those playwrights who literally "fall away from" the dangers of direct encounter with Shakespeare and take refuge in an alien but easily domesticated convention of

"Jacobean Decadence"

neoclassical melodrama with little more than sidelong glances at the native genius: such playwrights as Beaumont and Fletcher, Massinger, and Shirley, and not Tourneur, Middleton, Webster, and Ford. The attempt to reconstruct from within their work the poetic situations of these post-Shakespearean dramatists enables us to leave off chastising or excusing them for responding in their various ways to Shakespeare's strength, and to begin appreciating the different but no less authentic strength that derives from their deliberate choice *not* to be Shakespeare. For a self-conscious art is not synonymous with a decadent art, or all art would have to be decadent. Romantic bardolatry to the contrary, Shakespeare himself is not great because he is "natural" and un-self-conscious; he is, as I have tried to show, no less self-consciously artful than any of his successors and no more than he needs to be. Artistic self-consciousness is ultimately not a matter of degree that varies with chronology or culture, since it arises out of literature's constitutive, implicit, and inescapable, dependence on previous literature.

Many will no doubt continue to regard the major Jacobeans as more or less decadent offspring of Shakespeare and ascribe the changed nature of their theater to a changed Jacobean world, as if literature would not go on changing of its own inner restlessness even if the world did not. So deeply ingrained are the assumptions we bring to the study of literature that its essentially literary frame of reference is constantly repressed in favor of a wishful and naive mimeticism. Yet it is precisely the irrepressible impulse of literature to mock its own antecedents that enables it to defy entropy and render the concept of "decadence" irrelevant to its own history. Our study of the Jacobeans illustrates how literary history, unlike natural history, is imaginatively reconstituted anew with and within the work of every authentic writer, and must therefore remain a hypothetical and heuristic construct rather than an empirical record. Literature has always known this about itself, even if literary historians have not. It recognizes its temporal and cultural situation, as distinct from its poetic situation, as arbitrary, an empty coincidence which the literary historian may seize on as a starting-point in telling his own story, but only, if he is to remain true to the nature of literature, with the knowledge that it is a narrative convenience. In outlining my own story of the development of Elizabethan tragedy, I have tried not to reify its texts into historical events or documents and to suggest instead the ultimate atemporality of the relations between them, relations that could be illustrated, since they are "eterne in mutabilitie," in the literature of other languages, genres, and periods, earlier or later. That is another logical extension of the present work.

INDEX

Adelman, Janet, 108n, 110n
Adoration of the Shepherds, 124
Aeschylus, 145-46
allegory, in *Hamlet*, 46-52; in *King Lear*, 88-94; in *Macbeth*, 126-31; in *Othello*, 76-85; in *A Woman Killed with Kindness*, 152-53
archaism, 46-48, 50, 52; in *Hamlet*, 56-60; in *King Lear*, 92-99; in *Macbeth*, 137-39; in *The Revenger's Tragedy*, 160-67; in *A Woman Killed with Kindness*, 152-53
Ariosto, Lodovico, 18-20
Aristotle, 17, 34n, 39-40, 145-48
Auerbach, Erich, 39

Bacon, Francis, 39
Baker, Howard, 54n
Bale, John, *King Johan*, 70; *Three Laws*, 53
Barthes, Roland, 42
Bate, W. J., 14-15, 17, 38
Battenhouse, Roy, 77n
Baudelaire, Charles, 23, 25n
Beaumont and Fletcher, 60, 194
Bentley, G. E., 170n
Bloom, Harold, 14-17, 27n, 38
Boccaccio, Giovanni, 20, 119
Borges, Jorge Luis, 42
Bradley, A. C., 21, 73, 103, 111n, 112, 115n; on *King Lear*, 88, 90, 94n, 96n, 97
Brower, Reuben, 114
Burckhardt, Sigurd, 96n

Cambyses, 23, 70
Campbell, O. J., 88
Cervantes, Miguel de, 42

Chaucer, Geoffrey, 19-20
Coleridge, Samuel Taylor, 21, 39; as romantic interpreter, 86-87
Colie, Rosalie, 116n
Craik, T. W., 103n
Cunliffe, J. W., 54

Dante, 28
D'Avenant, Sir William, 139n, 142n
de Man, Paul, 12-13
demystification, in *Antony and Cleopatra*, 109-111; in *The Changeling*, 175; in *King Lear*, 105; in *Othello*, 81-86
Dent, R. W., 184n
Digby *Mary Magdalene*, 50
Digges, Leonard, 170n
Doran, Madeleine, 116n

Eliot, T. S., 75, 85-86, 170n, 171; on *Hamlet*, 49, 54n, 56-57; on *The Revenger's Tragedy*, 160, 164; on *A Woman Killed with Kindness*, 150-51
Elton, W. R., 88
Euripides, 146-48
evolutionary literary history, 21-23, 25, 57-58, 145-50

Ford, John, 148, 160, 169; *Perkin Warbeck*, 191-93; *'Tis Pity She's a Whore*, 192-93
Frost, David, 170n, 184
Frye, Northrop, 41n, 139n

Garrick, David, 142n
Giamatti, A. Bartlett, 19n
Gorboduc, 97
Guillén, Claudio, 25

197

Index

Harrowing of Hell, 121
Hartman, Geoffrey, 12-13
Harvey, Gabriel, 17
Hazlitt, William, 16
Hesiod, 30n, 34n
Heywood, John, 47, 121
Heywood, Thomas, 171; *A Woman Killed with Kindness*, 75-76, 151-57
Holinshed, Raphael, 87, 137n
Homer, 24, 28-29, 42; *Iliad*, 3, 34-37, 113; *Odyssey*, 30-34, 38
Horace, 23-24, 40-41
Horestes, 63
Hugo, Victor, 87
Hunter, G. K., 54n, 150
Hurd, Richard, 19

Ibsen, Henrik, 62
imitation, 39-42
influence, 13-21

Johnson, Samuel, 15-16, 61, 66, 81, 87
Jonson, Ben, 17, 19, 41, 44, 46, 170

Keats, John, 23, 24, 29, 31
Kernan, Alvin, 77n, 96n, 139n
King Leir, 87, 89
Kyd, Thomas, 161; *The Spanish Tragedy*, 48, 53, 157-58

Lamb, Charles, 21, 148
Levin, Harry, 23
Levin, Richard, 96n, 151n
Lord, Albert, 29
Lydgage, John, 119

Mack, Maynard, 57, 89-90, 103, 111n
Mack, Maynard, Jr., 139n
madness, in *Hamlet*, 50, 62; in *King Lear*, 100-102; in *Macbeth*, 131-32; in *The White Devil*, 184-86
Magnificence, 70
Mallarmé, Stephane, 32-33
Marlowe, Christopher, 23, 27-28, 42, 139, 148, 157-58, 192; *Dido*, 28; *Dr. Faustus*, 26, 119, 142, 159, 192; *Edward II*, 142, 159; *Tamburlaine*, 23, 26, 142
Massacre of the Innocents, 122
McGinn, Donald J., 164n
Middleton, Thomas, 148, 160, 171; *The Changeling*, 171-78
Milton, John, 15, 17-21, 24, 27-28, 42
mimesis, in *The Changeling*, 178; in *Hamlet*, 66; and modernity, 3-10; and the play-within-a-play, 69-74; in subplot of *A Woman Killed with Kindness*, 152 ff; theory of, 33, 38-43. *See also* imitation, representation
Mirror for Magistrates, 89, 92, 119
Miskimin, Alice S., 19n
modernity, 66, 98, 102, 142, 178; in Shakespearean criticism, 86-90; theory of, 3-10
morality play, and *Antony and Cleopatra*, 107-110; and *Hamlet*, 46-65; and *Henry IV*, 70-71; and *King Lear*, 91-94; and *Macbeth*, 142-43; and Marlowe, 26, 158-59; and *Othello*, 74-85; and *The Revenger's Tragedy*, 160-69; and *The Spanish Tragedy*, 157-58; and *A Woman Killed with Kindness*, 152-57. *See also* allegory
Mucedorus, 68

organicism, 57-58, 145-50

198

Index

ostranenie, 42

Page, Denys, 34n
Parry, Adam, 36-37
Parry, Milman, 29
Petrarchanism, in *Othello*, 84-85; in *Romeo and Juliet*, 114-15
Plato, 39
Plutarch, 113
Pope, Alexander, 38
post-modernism, 6-7
Pride of Life, 97
Proclus, 30

Racine, Jean, 41
Rare Triumphs of Love and Fortune, 68
representation, 3, 7-8, 40-41, 76, 84-86, 186. *See also* imitation, mimesis
Respublica, 53, 70
Rilke, Rainer Maria, 33
Romanticism, 13-15, 24; in Shakespearean criticism, 86-88; in Shakespeare's followers, 178, 186-91, 194
Rymer, Thomas, 85

Salingar, L. G., 160, 163
Sanders, Wilbur, 136n, 138n
Satire of the Three Estates, 53
Schiller, Friedrich von, 15, 29
Schlegel, Friedrich von, 15
Seneca, 54-55, 142
Shakespeare, William, *Antony and Cleopatra*, 106-112; *Coriolanus*, 113-14; *Hamlet*, 44-67; *Henry IV*, 58-59, 70-73; *Henry V*, 70; *Julius Caesar*, 105-106; *King Lear*, 87-105; *Love's Labor's Lost*, 69; *Macbeth*, 118-44; *Midsummer Night's Dream*, 68-69; *Othello*, 74-86; *Richard II*, 59; *Richard III*, 59, 119-20; *Romeo and Juliet*, 114-15; *Titus Andronicus*, 106; *Troilus and Cressida*, 109
Shklovsky, Victor, 42
Sidney, Sir Philip, 16-18, 46, 92
Soliman and Perseda, 48
Sophocles, 3, 40, 145-48
Spenser, Edmund, 16-19, 87
Spivack, Bernard, 57-59, 75, 86
Steadman, John, 24n
Steane, J. B., 139n
Stoll, Elmer Edgar, 21
sublation, 27-28, 39-42, 66, 173. *See also* representation
symbolism, 33, 38

Tasso, Torquato, 19
Tennyson, Alfred Lord, 43
Tourneur, Cyril, 148, 160; *The Revenger's Tragedy*, 160-69
Trilling, Lionel, 3-5
True Tragedy of Richard III, 47-48

Ur-Hamlet, 48, 55

verisimilitude, 39-40
Virgil, 16, 18, 20, 24, 26, 28-32, 38, 113-14
Visit of the Magi, 122

Ward, A. W., 172n
Warning for Fair Women, 155
Warren, Austin, 12
Webster, John, 148-50, 160, 169; *The Duchess of Malfi*, 188-91; *The White Devil*, 179-88
Wellek, René, 12
Wickham, Glynne, 120-21, 125-26
Wisdom, Who Is Christ, 51, 103n
Wordsworth, William, 24, 40-41

Library of Congress Cataloging in Publication Data

Felperin, Howard.
    Shakespearean representation.

    Includes index.
    1. Shakespeare, William, 1564-1616—Tragedies.
2. English drama—17th century—History and criticism.
3. Mimesis in literature. 4. Influence (Literary, artistic, etc.)
I. Title.
PR2983.F4   822.3'3   77-71982
ISBN 0-691-06341-9

GPSR Authorized Representative: Easy Access System Europe - Mustamäe tee
50, 10621 Tallinn, Estonia, gpsr.requests@easproject.com

www.ingramcontent.com/pod-product-compliance
Lightning Source LLC
Chambersburg PA
CBHW051523230426
43668CB00012B/1721